A
Student's
Guide
to History

Sixth Edition

Jules R. Benjamin
Ithaca College

St. Martin's Press • New York

Editor: Louise H. Waller
Manager, publishing services: Emily Berleth
Publishing services associate: Kalea Chapman
Project management: Chestnut Hill Enterprises, Inc.
Art direction: Sheree Goodman
Cover design: David Bamford
Cover photo: Paul Dunn/Tony Stone Images

For information, write:
St. Martin's Press, Inc.
175 Fifth Avenue
New York, NY 10010

ISBN: 0-312-08432-3

Acknowledgments

Reprinted from *The Marked Men* by Aris Fakinos, translated by Jacqueline
Lapidus, by permission of Liveright Publishing Corporation. Copyright ©
Aris Fakinos pour le texte grec. Copyright © 1969 Editions du Seuil. English
translation copyright © 1971 by Liveright Publishing Corporation.

L.S. Stavrianos, *The World Since 1500: A Global History*, 4th
edition, © 1982, p. 419. Reprinted by permission of Prentice Hall,
Inc., Englewood Cliffs, NJ.

Book review by Jonathan C. Brown in "Business History Review," 53
(Spring 1979), 144–145, reprinted by permission of the Harvard
Business School.

For Elaine, Aaron, and Adam

Preface:
To the Student

The aim of this book is to introduce you to the study of history and to assist you in history courses. Whether you are studying world history, Western civilization, ancient history, modern history, European history, United States history, British history, Canadian history, or another historical subject, this volume presents some basic concepts and methods of the field and helps you acquire the skills you will need in your work. The revisions in the sixth edition reflect the suggestions of students and teachers who have used the fifth edition. It is hoped that these changes will make the book even more useful to you.

The first chapter discusses the purposes and uses of historical study and explains how historians investigate their subjects. A discussion of the various schools of historical interpretation is included, along with an examination of some of the new directions and methods of historical research. It also tells you how the study of history helps prepare you for a variety of careers. Chapters 2 and 3 explain how to read a history assignment, take notes in class, study for exams, and organize and write a book report or essay exam. Sample book reviews are included, as is a section on reading maps, charts, graphs, and tables. The fourth and fifth chapters treat a more complex matter—preparing and writing a research paper. These chapters help you choose a topic, use the library to gather information, organize your research, and present the results of your work in your paper. There is a model term paper that shows you how the techniques discussed are actually applied. These chapters also contain advice for writing your own family history.

The appendices contain reference sources and general information that you will find useful both in your present course and in any other history courses you may take later on. The appendices have been expanded and revised as in each previous edition.

Throughout the book, it should be clear that the study of history is not an idle journey into a dead past, but an aid to understanding and living in the present. The basic ideas and tools introduced here should help you make use of history to answer important questions about your own life and your relationship to the world. This use, in the end, is what makes history valuable.

JULES R. BENJAMIN

Contents

chapter **1**

The Subject of History
and How to Use It

What Historians Are Trying to Do

Since the time when human beings invented writing, they have left records of their understanding of the world and of the events in their lives and how they felt about them. By studying the records that previous generations have left, we can find out about the kind of lives they led and how they faced their problems. We can use what we learn about the experiences of people who lived before us to help solve problems we face today. Though the modern world is quite different from the societies in which our ancestors lived, the story of their accomplishments and failures is the only yardstick by which we can measure the quality of our own lives and the success of our social arrangements.

All of us look into the past from time to time. We read historical novels or books about historical events. We gaze at old photographs or listen to the stories our grandparents tell. Historians, however, make a serious and systematic study of the past and attempt to use the knowledge they gain to help explain human nature and contemporary affairs. Professional historians spend their lives pursuing the meaning of the past for the present. To amateurs, historical research is like a hobby, but their occasional journeys into the past may contribute to the store of human knowledge and can greatly influence their own lives. Your study and research as a student qualify you as an amateur historian. Your study of the past is part of the same search for knowledge carried on generation after generation.

What History Can Tell You

Everything that exists in the present has come out of the past, and no matter how new and unique it seems to be, it carries some of the past with it. The latest hit recording by the newest group is the result of the evolution of that group's musical style and of the trends in music and society that have influenced them. Perhaps their style developed from earlier rock styles associated with the Beatles, or perhaps they are taking off from even older folk themes used by Bob Dylan. Well, Dylan was influenced by Woody Guthrie, who wrote his songs in the 1930s and whose music grew out of his contact with the heritage of American folk music from the nineteenth century, which in turn had come in great measure from earlier music in England and Scotland, some of which has its origins in the Middle Ages. Modern jazz, such as that of Billie Holiday or Louis Armstrong, evolved from the music of black communities in the United States and the Caribbean. Enslaved black people brought the earlier forms of that music with them from Africa in the eighteenth and nineteenth centuries. So you can see that the house of the present is filled with windows into the past.

The car you ride in, although it may have been designed only a few years ago, carries within it the basic components of the "horseless carriage" of the turn of the century. Your car works because people who knew how to make carriages, bicycles, and engines put their ideas together in a new way. The knowledge necessary to make the carriages and bicycles came, in turn, from earlier inventions. Some, like the wheel, go back into the antiquity of human history.

Everything has a history. At least part of the answer to any question about the contemporary world can come from studying the circumstances that led up to it. The problem is to find those past events, forces, arrangements, ideas, or facts that had the greatest influence on the present subject you have questions about. The more you understand about these past influences, the more you will know about the present subject to which they are related.

History and the Everyday World

Most of us are curious. Children are always asking their parents the "why" of things. When we grow up, we continue to ask questions because we retain our fascination with the mysteriousness and complexity of the world. Because everything has a history, most questions can be answered, at least in part, by historical investigation.

What are some of the things about which you are curious? Have you ever wondered why women's skirts in old movies are so long, or why French men often embrace one another whereas English men almost never do? Perhaps you have wondered how the Kennedy or Rockefeller families came to be rich, or why the Japanese attacked Pearl Harbor. Have you thought about why most of the peoples of southern Europe are Catholic whereas most northern Europeans are not? Many Asian peoples bow when they greet one another; we shake hands. The questions could go on forever; the answers are written somewhere in the record of the past.

The record of the past is not only contained in musty volumes on library shelves; it is all around us in museums, historical preservations, and the antique furnishings and utensils contained in almost every household. Our minds are living museums because the ideas we hold (for example, democracy, freedom, equality, competitiveness) have come down to us by way of a long historical journey. Though we are usually unaware of it, the past is always with us. Because history is literally at our fingertips, we can travel back into it without difficulty.

A Brief Journey into the Past

If you have ever driven any distance, you have probably ridden over a system of very modern superhighways with high speed limits and no cross traffic or stoplights. This national highway network, begun in the 1950s, connects all the major United States cities and is known as the interstate system. These roads were planned by the Eisenhower Administration in 1955, and, though they are the newest highways in the country, they have a history that is almost four decades long.

Looking for the marks of history in the world around us is something like the task of the geologist or archeologist. However, instead of digging down into the earth to uncover the past, the historical researcher digs into the visible, everyday elements of society to find the historical roots from which they sprang. The fact that the interstate highway system built in the 1960s and 1970s had its origins in the 1950s is just, so to speak, the uppermost layer of history. If a study of the newest highways can take us back thirty years, what about the historical roots of the older highways or of the country roads? How far into the past can we travel on them?

Turn off the eight-lane interstate, past the gleaming Exxon station, past the drive-up window of Burger King, past the bright signs before the multistoried Holiday Inn, and onto, say, U.S. Route 51 or 66. These are older highways, built mostly in the 1940s and 1950s. Being from an earlier period, like older strata of rock, perhaps they can tell us something of life in an earlier period of America.

When you leave the interstate system for this older road network, you first notice that the speed limit is lower and that many of the buildings are older. As you ride along at the slower pace, there are no signs saying "Downtown Freeway ½ mile" or "Indiana Turnpike—Exit 26N." They say "Lubbock 38 miles," or "Cedar Rapids 14 miles." As you approach Lubbock or Cedar Rapids, you will see motels less elaborate than the Holiday Inn. They may be small wooden cottages with fading paint and perhaps a sign that says "Star Motor Court" or "Stark's Tourist Cabins." Instead of Burger King or McDonald's, you may pass "Betty's Restaurant" or "Little River Diner." If you pay close attention to these buildings and do not become distracted by the more modern structures between them, you can take a trip into history even as you ride along. All of the older restaurants, stores, and gas stations you see were built before the large shopping centers and parking lots that separate them, and they are clues to the history of the highway on which you are riding. Places like the Star Motor Court and the Little River Diner probably were built when the road was new. Unless they have been modernized, they are relics of a previous historical period—when men named Roosevelt and Truman were president and when the cars that rode by looked like balloons with their big rounded hoods, trunks, and fenders. The diner isn't air-conditioned, and the sign over the tourist cabins proudly proclaims that they are "heated." This is the world of the 1930s and 1940s.

Now turn off the highway at State Route 104 where the sign says "Russell Springs 3 miles" or where it says "Hughesville 6 miles." Again the speed limit drops, and the bright colors fade farther away. You are on a road that may have been built in the 1920s or 1930s or earlier (in older sections of America, the country roads can go back a hundred years or more). Time has removed many of the buildings that once stood along this road, but if you look closely, the past is there ready to speak to you. The gas station here has only one set of pumps, and the station office sells bread, eggs, and kerosene. The faded advertisements on the wall display some products that you may have never heard of—NeHi Orange and Red Man Chewing Tobacco. If you see a restaurant or motel, it may be boarded up because the people who used to stop in on their way to Russell Springs or Hughesville now go another way or may no longer live in the country but in a nearby city. However, many of the homes along Route 104 are still there. They were built when only farmland straddled the road, and they may go back to a time when horses and not internal combustion engines pulled the traffic past the front door. Such relics of early technology as old washing machines and refrigerators may stand on the tilting wooden porches, and a close look behind the tall weeds beside the dirt driveway may reveal the remains of a 1936 La Salle. As you stop before one of the old farmhouses, the past is all around you, and, although the place does not appear in its youthful form, a little imagination can reconstruct what life was like here on the day in 1933 when Roosevelt closed all the banks or the day in 1918 when the Great War in Europe ended.

The line linking past to present never breaks, and the house itself has a history, as do the people who once lived in it. In this sense, every house is haunted with its own past, and a keen eye can see the signs. Enter the house and you can see the stairway that was rebuilt in 1894, and in the main bedroom upstairs the fireplace, which was put in about 1878, the year the house was built. Perhaps the old Bible on the table near the bed notes the year the family came to the United States, and the dates in the early nineteenth century when the parents of the immigrants who built the house were born.

The story could go on forever, although the evidence would become slimmer and slimmer. You could find out from county records who owned the land before the house was built, going back perhaps to the time when the people who lived on the land were American Indians. In distance you may have traveled only ten or twenty miles from the interstate highway and it may have taken you less than an hour, but by looking for the signs of the past in the present, you have traveled more than a hundred years into history.

If you think and study about the passage of time between the old farmhouse on the country road and the gleaming service station by the interstate, you may come to understand some of the social, political, and economic forces that moved events away from the old wooden porch and sent them speeding down the interstate highway. The more you know about this process, the more you will learn about the times when the farmhouse was new and the more you will understand how the interstate highway came about, what you are doing riding on it, and into what kind of a future you may be heading.

Historians don't usually wander into history in such a casual fashion. They have to be trained in their methods of investigation and analysis. As an introduction to your own historical research and study, the next section will describe some of the tools employed by historians in their examination of the records of the past.

How Historians Work

Like you, historians are challenged by the complexity of the world, and many want to use their studies of the past to help solve the problems of the present. The questions that can come to mind are numberless, and serious historical investigators must choose wisely among them. They do not want to spend a lot of effort pursuing the kind of question to which history has no answer (for example, "What is the purpose of the Universe?" "Am I a lovable person?" "Who is the smartest person in the world?"). Nor do they want to struggle to achieve the solution to a problem that is not of real importance. (Historical investigation can probably tell you who wore the first pair of pants with a zipper in it, but that might not be worth knowing.) The main difficulty facing historians is not eliminating unanswerable or unimportant questions but choosing among the important ones.

A historian's choice among important questions is determined by personal values, by the concerns of those who support the historian's work, by the nature of the time in which the historian lives, or by a combination of all of these. The ways in which these influences operate are very complex, and often historians themselves are unaware of them.

When the historian has chosen his or her subject, many questions still remain. For example, does historical evidence dealing with the subject exist, and if so, where can it be found? If someone wanted to study gypsy music from medieval Europe, and that music was never written down or mentioned in historical accounts of the period, then little or nothing can be found about this subject through historical research. Even if records exist on a particular subject, the historian may be unaware of them or unable to locate them. Perhaps the records are in an unfamiliar language or are in the possession of individuals or governments that deny access to them. Sometimes locating historical evidence can be a problem.

Having determined that records *do* exist and that they can be located and used, the historian faces another and more important problem: What is the credibility or reliability of the evidence? Is it genuine? How accurate are the records, and what biases were held by those who wrote them? If sources of information are in conflict, which is correct? Or is it possible that most of the sources are in error? Historians must pick and choose among the sources they uncover, and that is not always easy to do. The historian's own biases also cloud the picture, making impartial judgment extremely difficult.

There are two basic forms of historical evidence: primary and secondary. Primary evidence records the actual words of someone who participated in or witnessed the events described. These can be newspaper accounts, diaries, notebooks, letters, minutes, interviews, and any works written by persons who claim firsthand knowledge of an event. Another primary source is official statements by established organizations or significant personages—royal decrees, church edicts, political party platforms, laws, and speeches. Recent history has been recorded by photographs, films, and audio- and videotapes. These recordings of events as they actually happened are also primary forms of evidence. Artifacts are another form of primary evidence. These are things made by people in the past: houses, public buildings, tools, clothing, and much more.

Secondary evidence records the findings of someone who did not observe the event but who investigated primary evidence. Most history books fall into this category, although some are actually tertiary evidence because they rely not on primary evidence but are themselves drawn from secondary sources. When your own history research paper is finished, it will be secondary or, more likely, tertiary evidence to anyone who may use it in the future.

The problem of determining the reliability of evidence is a serious one. Secondary and even primary evidence can be fraudulent, inaccurate, or biased. Eyewitness accounts may be purposely distorted in order to avert blame or to bestow praise on a particular individual or group. Without intending to misinform, even on-the-scene judgments can be incorrect. Sometimes, the closer you are to an event, the more emotionally involved you are, and this distorts your understanding of it. We can all recall events in which we completely misunderstood the feelings, actions, and even words of another person. Historians have to weigh evidence carefully to see if those who have participated in an event understood it well enough to accurately describe it, and whether later authors understood the meaning of the primary documents they used. Official statements present another problem—that of propaganda or concealment. A government, group, or institution may make statements that it wishes others to believe but that are not true. What a group says may not be what it does. This is especially true in politics.

To check the reliability of evidence, historians use the tests of consistency and corroboration: does the evidence contradict itself and does it agree with evidence from other sources? Historical research always involves checking one source against another.

The bias of a source also presents difficulties. People's attitudes toward the world influence the way they interpret events. For example, you and your parents may have different attitudes toward music, sex, religion, or politics. These differences can cause you to disagree with them about the value of a rock concert, a Sunday sermon, or the president. Historians have their own attitudes toward the subjects they are investigating, and these cause them to draw different conclusions about the character and importance of religious, political, intellectual, and other movements. Later historians must take these biases into account when weighing the reliability of evidence.

In analyzing the evidence, the historian must find some way of organizing it so that he or she can make clear its meaning. A mass of facts and opinions concerning a subject is not a historical study. The task of the trained historian is to arrange the material so that it supports a particular conclusion. This conclusion may have been in the historian's mind at the outset, or it might be the result of investigation. If the evidence does not appear to support the conclusion, however, then the historian must either change that conclusion or seek other evidence to support it.

Once a historian is satisfied that research has uncovered sufficient evidence to support a particular conclusion, then he or she works to display the evidence in a manner that will clearly show that the conclusion drawn is a proper one. If any evidence that leads to other conclusions is uncovered, the historian has a responsibility to include it. In doing so, he or she must show how the supporting evidence is stronger than the nonsupporting evidence. There are many ways of organizing evidence in support of a conclusion. The historian's arguments in favor of a particular conclusion must be strong and convincing, and the logic of these arguments must not be faulty.

Recently, in an effort to address the problems of error, bias, and faulty logic as much as possible, some historians have turned to techniques from mathematics and science to handle historical evidence and test conclusions. These historians prefer to deal with quantitative or uniform data that are easily comparable and that can be interpreted by mathematical formulas. Such researchers often use computers to analyze their data. They question historical findings involving opinion and judgment and look to types of evidence (usually statistical) that they believe can test the more intuitive conclusions of other historians. The kinds of problems they deal with are usually narrow, and they have to be well trained in techniques of statistical analysis. Their tests of evidence are sophisticated and are becoming more so. The extent to which the study of history can or should become "scientific" is an important debate among historians.

Traditional Directions of Historical Research

Historians investigate the questions they choose to study in many ways. Their particular approach depends on their values and experiences, their academic training, and their belief about which aspects of human nature and the human environment are most important to an understanding of their subject. Traditionally, historians have been divided into those who saw social, cultural, intellectual, political, diplomatic, economic, or psychological matters as central to answering the question being investigated. The social historian investigates the development of human groups and communities and their interactions with the larger society from which they emerge. The cultural and intellectual historian deals with the meaning of ideas and attitudes and their relationship to social changes. The political historian focuses on the operation and acts of governments, parties, and institutions, whereas diplomatic historians deal with relations between governments. The economic historian studies developments in technology, production, consumption, and the division of wealth.

For the most part, scholars working in traditional fields of social, cultural, intellectual, political, diplomatic, and economic history gather their materials from the written record (both primary and secondary) and present their findings in the form of a narrative. As in a historical novel, this narrative tells the story of the important structures, events, personalities, or changes that have been researched. The goal of this form of historical writing is to re-create a part of the past so that it will appear as real as it once did to those who lived through it and yet will explain the meaning of events from the vantage point of the present, when the outcome of the historical events has become more clear. One of the most common forms of narrative history is biography: the story of the life and times of an important person.

New Directions of Historical Research

In recent years, some historians have begun to explore different aspects of the past. Psychohistorians are examining the emotional development of individuals, families, and even groups. They attempt to explain some part of people's actions and thoughts as the result of the inner workings of their minds and their emotional reactions to important social developments such as wars, depressions, and class and ethnic conflict. Another new direction is the history of science and technology. Here the focus is on the evolution of scientific knowledge, how such knowledge arises and how its application influences society. Historical demography, the study of statistics concerning the numbers and distribution of populations and the social impact of population changes, is another new direction. Ethnohistory is a branch of cultural history that studies individual cultures (or the contact between different cultures) in order to trace the causes of cultural change. Environmental historians examine the interaction of human communities with their habitats.

Another new field of research is the study of private life, a subject that has surprising historical significance. This field includes family history, sports history, film history, the history of childhood, and parts of the rapidly growing and influential study of women's history.

Some of the new directions are reorientations of traditional fields of historical research. Thus, there are now the fields of "new" social history as well as "new" political and "new" economic history. Some scholars in these fields prefer to look beneath the broad developments studied by the more traditionally oriented historians to find evidence of group behavior: voting patterns, group memberships, religious affiliations, standards of living, etc. This evidence is used to establish an understanding of basic aspects of life in the past and to test the accuracy of assumptions made by scholars working with more impressionistic evidence: diaries, public speeches, novels, contemporary histories, political events, etc.

Two of the "new" directions of research are in fact quite old: genealogy and local history. These fields have returned to importance as people have become concerned with holding on to or rediscovering their personal, family, or neighborhood past. Genealogy is a branch of the larger (and more scholarly) study of family history. It concerns itself with tracing the ancestry of a particular individual. Local history, engaged in with enthusiasm and affection by residents and scholars alike, examines the evolution of a town, a community, or a neighborhood.

New Methods of Historical Research

Many of the new directions of historical research have been influenced by other fields of knowledge: psychohistory by psychology, demography and the new social history by sociology, ethnohistory by anthropology, the new political history by political science, the new economic history by economics. While still adhering to the special focus of history—examining and explaining the past—historians working in these new areas often borrow ideas and methods of analyzing evidence from these other fields. These scholars make use of quantitative data—that is, information about the past such as election returns, price levels, and population statistics—to re-create a picture of earlier times. Because quantitative data is uniform, it measures the same things—votes, prices, numbers of inhabitants—over time. Thus, comparisons can be made among statistics from different periods. The electoral support of a political party, the price of wheat, or the size of a town can be examined to see if it is rising or falling and at what rate.

If the uniformity of the data can be established (that is, if the numbers really *do* measure the same thing in each time period), then they can be subjected to mathematical analysis. Percentages, ratios, averages, the mean, median, and mode can be obtained. If the data set is large, the historian may subject it to more complex analyses that explore patterns within the numbers and among subgroups of them: the frequency distribution, the standard deviation, and the coefficient of variation. The more elaborate kinds of statistical analysis can determine not merely how fast prices are rising or where the majority of a party's voters reside; they also can compare different kinds of changes—party registration with price levels, population decline with employment levels—in an attempt to describe the conditions under which certain changes occur. By noting those categories of numbers (variables) that move together, the historian can begin to explore the causes of the changes under examination.

Elaborate analysis of statistics and the examination of large bodies of data (millions of voters, prices, households) are made possible by the use of computers that count as well as track changes in and compare immense amounts of evidence. To make such analyses, the computer must be programmed—that is, provided with detailed instructions on how to handle the data. It is vital that the information fed into the computer be uniform. Each unit must represent the same thing—votes, dollars' worth of wheat, households, etc. Numbers representing the price of wheat per bushel cannot be entered into the computer in the same category as wheat per pound. These two sets of data are not uniform and cannot be compared. If you tell the computer to add apples and oranges, it will do so, but the result will have no meaning.

The computer is not only a means of analyzing historical data, it is also becoming important as a way of gathering historical facts. Even more significant, it can make these facts available to students at all levels. History *databases*, containing millions of individual historical statistics, are often found in college libraries. Data on shipping from Liverpool, England, to Boston in 1839 or on the size of the Texas cotton crop in 1920 can be made instantly available. (For a list of history databases, see Appendix A, section XI.)

Schools of Historical Interpretation

Historical investigation can lead to very different results depending upon the aspect of human nature or society emphasized and the kind of information obtained. Even greater differences can result from historical investigations that employ different *philosophies* of history.

A philosophy of history is an explanation not only of the most important causes of specific events but of the broadest developments in human affairs. It explains the *forces* of history, what moves them, and in what direction they are headed. The dominant philosophy of history of a particular age is that which most closely reflects the beliefs and values of that age. Most of the historians writing at that time will write from the perspective of that philosophy of history.

We will look now at some of the principal philosophies of history, those which have prevailed over long periods of civilization.

Perhaps the oldest philosophy of history is the *cyclical* one. According to this view, events recur periodically. This school holds the belief, in short, that history repeats itself. The essential forces of nature and of human nature are changeless, causing past patterns of events to repeat themselves endlessly. As the saying goes, "There is nothing new under the sun." This view of history was dominant from ancient times until the rise of Christianity. The Aztecs conceived of history this way, as did the Chinese.

A central message of early Christianity was the uniqueness of the life, death, and resurrection of Jesus Christ. In societies influenced by the Christian Church—and especially in Europe in the Middle Ages—the new concept of divine intervention to overthrow the past weakened the cyclical view.[1] The resulting philosophy of history, the *providential school*, held that the course of history was determined by God. The ebb and flow of historical events represent struggles between forces of good and evil. These struggles are protracted, but the eventual victory of good is foreseen.

This particular idea of the providential school—that history is characterized not by ceaseless repetition but by direction and purpose—became an element in the thinking of the more secular age beginning with the eighteenth century. In this new age of scientific inquiry and material advancement, there arose the *progressive school*, whose central belief was that human history illustrates neither endless cycles nor divine intervention but continual progress. According to this school, the situation of humanity is constantly improving. Moreover, this improve-

---

[1]An earlier development of this new view is found in the Old Testament.

ment results not from divine providence but from the efforts of human beings themselves. Each generation builds upon the learning and improvements of those preceding it and, in doing so, reaches a higher stage of civilization. This idea of history as continual progress is still very powerful today.[2] Currently, many variations of the progressive philosophy share the field of historical investigation. Should you be interested in this subject, your instructor will be able to introduce you to the field of historiography (the study of the methods and interpretations of historians) and to the works of philosophers of history themselves.

What You Can Do with History

It is said that experience is the best teacher. Still, our learning would be very narrow if we profited only from our own experiences. Through the reading of history, we make other people's experiences our own. In this way, we touch other times and places and add to our lifetime's knowledge that gained by others.

If history is the greatest teacher, what can we do with the knowledge we draw from it? In what practical ways does knowledge of the past help us to accomplish the work we do? Perhaps you wait on customers at McDonald's or are the manager of a bank. Will knowledge acquired in history courses be of direct value to you? Probably not. You can serve burgers and fries satisfactorily without knowing that the Safavid empire of the sixteenth century was located in Persia. You can run a bank without knowledge of the philosophy of John Locke. However, while the bank manager can run the bank without *particular* historical knowledge, he or she cannot do so without writing reports summarizing the financial transactions of the bank over time. To write such reports, the manager must have mastered the skills of historical research. Though reports to the bank's president deal only with the past week's or month's transactions at the branch rather than with past years or centuries, the manager must gather evidence, analyze and summarize it, and draw conclusions about it, just as would the historian whose subject is the hundred-year history of the bank.

History is not merely a course you take in college; it is a way of thinking about the present, one that attempts to make sense of the complexity of contemporary events by examining what lies behind them. Such an examination is intellectual (its goal is to broaden understanding in general), but it can be practical as well. If business at the branch bank

---

[2]One of the most influential of the progress theories is the dialectical materialism of Karl Marx.

falls off sharply in June, what is the manager to do? Does this mean that the branch should be closed? If the manager had no records of the bank's past performance, the question could not be answered. However, all businesses look at themselves over time and employ researchers and analysts to do so. Thus the manager has reports on the level of business done by the bank in years past. A study of these reports (similar to the primary evidence of the historian) makes it clear that business always drops in June because a major depositor, a nearby factory, shuts down then for retooling. The lesson is a simple one: no business can operate intelligently without an understanding of its own history. In a sense, the office workers in business, government, and institutions operate as historical record-producers and record-keepers. When decisions about policy or future production and investment are made, these records are pulled together in research reports that examine the past experience of the firm (or department or institution) in order to judge the likely result of these decisions.

While the ability to re-create the past is an important ingredient in enabling the bank manager to do a good job, there are many careers in which knowledge of historical research techniques is an essential requirement. Government agencies, large corporations, libraries, museums, labor unions, historical parks, monuments, and restorations all take knowledge of the past so seriously that they employ staffs of historians and archivists whose sole task is to conduct research, organize records, re-create historic buildings and events, and write histories. The fields of public and corporate history, museum and archival management, and historic restoration are only some of the areas that *directly* employ the skills you acquire when studying history in school.

When you learn how to read history, how to research the past, and how to write a summary of your findings, you are mastering career skills as surely as if you were taking a course in real-estate law or restaurant management. The ability to see the present in relationship to the past is a skill needed not only by academic and public historians, archivists, historical novelists, and documentary producers; it is an essential preparation for almost any career. Understanding the past can be its own reward, but it pays off in other ways as well. In fact, people who think that history is irrelevant run the risk of history making that judgment of them.

chapter 2

How to Read a History Assignment and Take Notes in Class

How to Read a History Assignment

Reading history can be a satisfying experience, but to enjoy the landscape you must first know where you are; that is, you must have a general sense of the subject and of the manner in which it is being presented. If you begin reading before you get your bearings, you may become lost in a forest of unfamiliar facts and interpretations. Before beginning any reading assignment, look over the entire book. Read the preface or introduction. This should tell you something about the author and his or her purpose in writing the work. Then read the table of contents to get a sense of the way in which the author has organized the subject. Next, skim the chapters themselves, reading subheadings and glancing at illustrations and graphed material. If you have the time, preread sections of the book (especially the introductory and concluding chapters) rapidly before reading the full work.

After you have scouted the ground, you will be ready to read. By this time, you should be familiar with the topic of the book (what generally it is all about), the background of the author (politician, journalist, historian, eyewitness, novelist, etc.), when it was written (a hundred-year-old classic, the newest book on the subject), how it is organized (chronologically, topically), and, most important of all, its thesis and conclusions. The thesis of a book is the principal point on the subject that the author wishes to make: that the geography of Spain was a principal factor in that nation's failure to industrialize in the eighteenth and nineteenth centuries; that disagreement on moral issues between J. Robert Oppenheimer and Edward Teller delayed development of the hydrogen bomb. Most authors set out their thesis in a preface or introduction. If you understand the principal point the author is trying to make, then the organization and conclusions of the work will become clear to you. The author will be organizing evidence and drawing conclusions to support the thesis. By the way, if the thesis is not clear or the evidence is not supportive of it, then it is not a good history of its subject no matter how many facts it contains. The ability to spot such weaknesses and describe them is part of learning history too. (See Chapter 3, the section on "Book Reviews.")

The most common history assignment is the reading of a textbook. Many students hope to get by with their lecture notes, and they put off reading the text until just before the final exam. Reading the text week by week will give you the background knowledge necessary to understand the lectures and supplementary readings. In most courses the lectures embellish portions of the text, and lecturers assume that students are familiar with it. Sitting through a lecture on the economic aspects of the American Revolution will be confusing if you have not read the textbook discussion of the mercantilist theories behind many of the colonists' grievances.

Read the text chapters in close conjunction with the lectures to which they are related. If you are not sure that you understand the material, read it again. Underline the most prominent factual information. Also underline important generalizations, interpretations, and conclusions. Of course, don't underline most of the book. That would be a sign that you cannot tell the difference between the author's main points and the material he or she uses to tie these points together. In addition to underlining, look for passages emphasized by the author or those which you feel reflect the author's viewpoint or with which you disagree. Write your reaction or a summary of the passages in the margin. All of this will come in handy when you prepare to take a test. You will be able to reread the underlined material and your comments and obtain a quick review of the chapter's contents. Before the final, however, you may need to reread the text itself, especially if you are having difficulty in the course or wish to write an outstanding exam.

Another typical reading assignment is a monograph (a specialized history work on a particular subject). In addition to the procedures used in reading a textbook, you will need to pay special attention to the theme and point of view of these works. They should be read more carefully because your teacher will expect you to learn not only about the subject they deal with but about the emphasis and methods of the work. Therefore, you will need to determine the author's assumptions and values, and to understand the book's thesis and conclusions. Read this kind of work not only to absorb the facts but also to analyze, question, and criticize. If you own the book, you can do your questioning and criticizing in the margins. If the book is not yours, or if you wish to have an organized set of notes about it, summarize the contents and the author's theme on index cards (4″ × 6″ or 5″ × 8″). You can then review your underlinings or index cards before the exam.

Some courses also involve the assignment of a book of readings. These are usually a series of short essays (excerpts from larger works or from primary documents) that deal with a single subject. All of the suggestions concerning the reading of texts and history books apply here as well, but this type of assignment often calls for a particular kind of reading. Each excerpt usually discusses a different aspect or interpretation of the subject, and some are in serious disagreement. Teachers expect students to be able to assess the arguments of the various writers and on occasion to take a position in the controversy. Therefore, you must read this particular kind of book with an eye to analyzing the arguments of the different excerpts or to comparing their different approaches to the subject. A good way to do this is to summarize briefly the argument or approach of each selection.

Still another reading assignment is a historical novel. This is a work of fiction based upon actual occurrences and people. It is more dramatic and more personal than a text or monograph and describes the feelings of those caught up in important historical events. Reading such a novel gives you a feel for the times that it conveys and for the historical material it contains, but be cautious not to treat it as historical truth. On the other hand, if the novelist knows the historical period or event well, he or she can make it come alive in ways that scholarly works cannot.

To help you appreciate the differences among the four types of reading assignments, here are passages from each. The subject is the Greek Civil War of the late 1940s and the role of the United States in that war. The textbook passage is from Stephen E. Ambrose, *Rise to Globalism: Ameri-*

can Foreign Policy Since 1938 (New York: Penguin, 1971), pp. 148 and
150. The monograph passage is from Joyce and Gabriel Kolko, *The
Limits of Power: The World and United States Foreign Policy, 1945–1954*
(New York: Harper & Row, 1972), p. 341. The readings passage is from
an address delivered by President Harry Truman before a joint session of
Congress on March 12, 1947. The final passage is from the historical
novel *The Marked Men* by Aris Fakinos (New York: Liveright, 1971), pp.
92–93. As you read these passages, note the different manner in which
each deals with this subject.

Textbook
The day before, 6 March, Truman had begun to prepare
the ground. In a speech at Baylor University in Texas he
explained that freedom was more important than peace and
that freedom of worship and speech were dependent on
freedom of enterprise. . . .
The State Department, meanwhile, was preparing a message for Truman to deliver to the full Congress. He was
unhappy with the early drafts, for "I wanted no hedging in
this speech. This was America's answer to the surge of expansion of Communist tyranny. It had to be clear and free of
hesitation or double talk." Truman told Acheson to have the
speech toughened, simplified, and expanded to cover more
than just Greece and Turkey. He then made further revisions in the draft. . . .
At 1 P.M. on 12 March 1947, Truman stepped to the
rostrum in the hall of the House of Representatives to address the joint session of the Congress. The speech was also
carried on nationwide radio. He asked for immediate aid for
Greece and Turkey, then explained the reasoning. "I believe that it must be the policy of the United States to
support free peoples who are resisting attempted subjuga-
tion by armed minorities or by outside pressures."
The statement was all-encompassing. In a single sentence, Truman had defined American policy for the next
twenty years. Whenever and wherever an anti-Communist
government was threatened, by indigenous insurgents, foreign invasion, or even diplomatic pressure (as with Turkey),
the United States would supply political, economic, and
most of all, military aid. The Truman Doctrine came close
to shutting the door against any revolution, since the terms

"free peoples" and "anti-Communist" were assumed to be synonymous. All the Greek government, or any dictatorship, had to do to get American aid was to claim that its opponents were Communists. And the aid would be unilateral, as Truman never mentioned the United Nations, whose commission to investigate what was actually happening in Greece had not completed its study or made a report.

Monograph

What was really on the mind of the president and his advisers was stated less in the Truman Doctrine speech than in private memos and in Truman's March 6 address at Baylor University. Dealing with the world economic structure, the president attacked state-regulated trade, tariffs, and exchange controls—". . . the direction in which much of the world is headed at the present time." "If this trend is not reversed," he warned, ". . . the United States will be under pressure, sooner or later, to use these same devices in the fight for markets and for raw materials. . . . It is not the American way. It is not the way to peace."[16] . . .

The question of how best to sell the new crusade perplexed the administration, not the least because Greece was a paltry excuse for a vast undertaking of which it "was only a beginning," and in the end it formulated diverse reasons as the need required.[18] The many drafts that were drawn up before the final Truman Doctrine speech was delivered to Congress on March 12 are interesting in that they reveal more accurately than the speech itself the true concerns of Washington. Members of the cabinet and other top officials who considered the matter before the twelfth understood very clearly that the United States was now defining a strategy and budget appropriate to its new global commitments—interests that the collapse of British power had made even more exclusively American—and that far greater involvement in other countries was now pending, at least on the economic level.

Quite apart from the belligerent tone of the drafts were the references to ". . . a world-wide trend away from the system

---

[16]DSB, March 16, 1947, 484. See also Acheson, *Present at the Creation*, 219; Jones, *Fifteen Weeks*, 139–42.
[18]Acheson, *Present at the Creation*, 221.

of free enterprise toward state-controlled economies," which
the State Department's speech writers thought "gravely
threatened" American interests. No less significant was the
mention of the "great natural resources" of the Middle East
at stake.

Readings (excerpt from speech)
The very existence of the Greek state is today threatened
by the terrorist activities of several thousand armed men,
led by Communists, who defy the government's authority
at a number of points, particularly along the northern
boundaries. . . .

Meanwhile, the Greek Government is unable to cope
with the situation. The Greek army is small and poorly
equipped. It needs supplies and equipment if it is to restore
authority to the government throughout Greek territory.

Greece must have assistance if it is to become a self-
supporting and self-respecting democracy.

The United States must supply this assistance. . . .

At the present moment in world history nearly every
nation must choose between alternative ways of life. The
choice is too often not a free one.

One way of life is based upon the will of the majority,
and is distinguished by free institutions, representative
government, free elections, guarantees of individual lib-
erty, freedom of speech and religion, and freedom from
political oppression.

The second way of life is based upon the will of a minority
forcibly imposed upon the majority. It relies upon terror
and oppression, a controlled press and radio, fixed elections, and the suppression of personal freedoms.

I believe that it must be the policy of the United States to
support free peoples who are resisting attempted subjuga-
tion by armed minorities or by outside pressures. . . .

It is necessary only to glance at a map to realize that the
survival and integrity of the Greek nation are of grave importance in a much wider situation. If Greece should fall under
the control of an armed minority, the effect upon its neigh-
bor, Turkey, would be immediate and serious. Confusion
and disorder might well spread throughout the entire Middle East.

Moreover, the disappearance of Greece as an independent state would have a profound effect upon those countries in Europe whose peoples are struggling against great difficulties to maintain their freedoms and their independence while they repair the damages of war. . . .

The free peoples of the world look to us for support in maintaining their freedoms.

If we falter in our leadership, we may endanger the peace of the world—and we shall surely endanger the welfare of this Nation.

Great responsibilities have been placed upon us by the swift movement of events.

I am confident that the Congress will face these responsibilities squarely.

Historical Novel

Tzelekis was right: now it was 1949, and war was beautifully organized—things were done in an orderly fashion. Various specialists had come in, trained in "wars of movement": The British, the Americans, with a good deal of experience in such matters. They put things in their places, taught enemies and friends to recognize each other—you over here, them over there. Work with a system, no fooling around! Back in '46, you see, everything was topsy-turvy. The army was an indiscriminate herd, no organization whatever; everyone did as he pleased, everything pell-mell, all mixed up together slaughtering: EAM-ites, EDES-ites, X-ites—you didn't know who was your enemy and who your friend. At night they sent out patrols in the morning they came back in company with the others and cut up their captains. Other times when they fought at night with knives and bayonets it was like mother losing child and child losing mother: same clothes (all the rags of the world resemble each other), same appearance—you came face to face with the enemy, you went at him with a dagger to rip out his guts, and you saw—if you had time—that he was one of your own men, so you let him go and went for the one beside him. And don't forget, what mixed things up even worse was the language; since they were all spouting Greek, who could tell them apart? . . .

Later when foreign aid began to arrive, the army got new

uniforms, munitions, wireless transmitters, codes of recognition. Things were put in order, names were given to the enemy, and the radio blared them out every day, they were written on the walls and in the newspapers; and finally, for the first time in their history, the Greeks began to kill each other systematically. The solution was a very simple one; and a considerable number of people couldn't understand why they had not thought of it before.

Note that the textbook is general in its coverage. It does not use footnotes or quote from primary sources other than Truman's speech. It tries to summarize the content and meaning of the event without too much detail and without extensive proof for its conclusions. The monograph, on the other hand, covers a smaller portion of the topic, gives more detail, quotes from primary materials, and uses footnotes to record its sources of information. The selection from the book of readings is a primary source—the Truman speech itself. Often these books are composed of the original documents that form the basis of the historical events discussed by textbooks and monographs. Although this particular selection from a book of readings is a primary document, such works, as already noted, may also be collections of short essays or excerpts from monographs.

The section from the historical novel is very different from the first three passages. The author gives us the thoughts of some of the soldiers who fought in the Greek Civil War, far away from the formulation of foreign policy in Washington.

How to Read Maps, Charts, Graphs, and Tables

History is often displayed on maps. The landscape of history is one of its most fundamental settings. The rise and fall of empires, the course of wars, the growth of cities, the development of trade routes, and much more can be traced on maps of large areas. Map 1 (see page 24) indicates the dates on which parts of Africa came under European colonial rule. Map 2 (see page 25) indicates the dates on which the nations of Africa became independent. Small area maps can show the layout of villages, the outcome of battles, or the location of mines, canals, and railroads. To read a map, you must learn the *key*, which translates the symbols used on the map. A line on a map may be a road, a river, or a gas pipeline. The key tells you which it is. The *scale* of a map tells you the actual distance of the area the map represents. Maps are an important aid in understanding history because they display the physical relationship between places. Never ignore maps in a text or other reading. It is also wise to put a good map of the area you are studying near your desk so that you can see the location of places mentioned in lectures and readings.

In addition to maps, works in history often include statistical data arranged in charts, graphs, or tables. These data describe the amounts of something (e.g., warships, marriages, schools, bridges, deaths from smallpox) at a specific time in the past and usually compare these amounts (e.g., the number of marriages in relation to the number of schools) or trace changes in amounts over time (e.g., the number of warships in 1820, 1830, and 1840). The following are typical arrangements of statistical data with explanations as to how to read them.

Estimated World Population[1]
(Numbers represent millions of persons)

	1650	1750	1850	1900	1950	1977
Europe	100	140	265	400	570	740
United States and Canada	2	2	25	80	165	240
Latin America	12	10	35	65	165	340
Africa	100	95	95	120	220	425
Asia	330	480	750	940	1370	2355

[1] These are rough estimates only. The figures for 1650 and 1750 in particular come from a time before it was common to conduct a periodic count (*census*) of populations. There is a great debate about the size of the native populations of the Western hemisphere before 1850.

This table organizes population statistics from different regions of the earth and across more than three hundred years. Reading across the lines allows you to trace the changes in population of a particular region (Europe, Africa, Asia) over time. By doing so, you can follow the population of each region at hundred-year intervals (the population of Latin America in 1650, 1750, 1850, and 1950). You can note the change for each region and the rate of change. For example, the population of the United States and Canada did not increase in the hundred years between 1650 and 1750, whereas it more than doubled in the fifty years between 1900 and 1950. Reading down the chart, you can examine the population of each region during the same period in time. This allows you to compare the populations of the different regions. In 1650 the populations of Europe and Africa were the same, whereas in 1950 the European population was more than two-and-one-half times that of Africa.

More complex comparisons can be made by combining the differences between regions (reading down) and their rates of growth over time (reading across). For example, you can discover that whereas the population of Asia has grown more than that of any other region in absolute

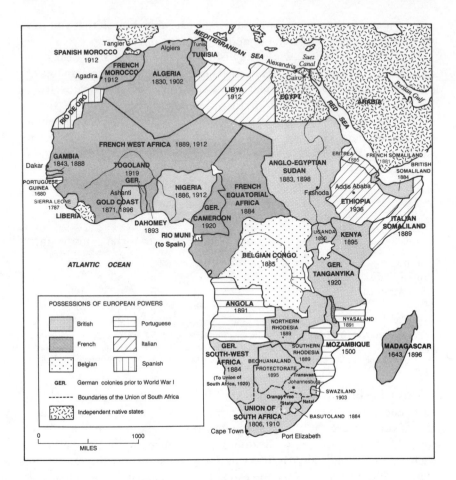

Map 1
The March of Colonialism in Africa

terms, its *rate* of growth from 1850 to 1977 (750 million to 2355 million, or about 300 percent) was much less than that of Latin America (35 million to 340 million, or almost 1,000 percent).

Even the cold statistics of a table can provide images of the great drama of history. The decrease in African population between 1650 and 1850 may tell us something of the impact of the slave trade, and the decrease in

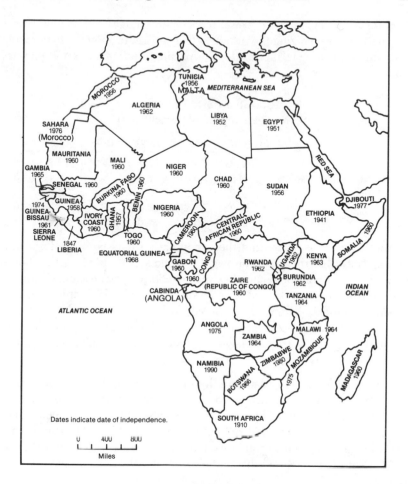

Map 2
The March of African Independence

population in Latin America between 1650 and 1750 hints at the toll taken among native Americans by the introduction of European diseases. The large increase in the United States population between 1850 and 1900 tells us something about the history of European immigration.

The information in the table can be presented differently in order to highlight different aspects of the data. In the following table, the numbers for each region are represented as percentages of the total world population. By changing the numbers from absolute amounts to percentages, the new table facilitates the comparing of populations and population growth.

Estimated World Population
(Numbers represent percentages)

	1650	1750	1850	1900	1950	1977
Europe	18.4	19.3	22.8	25.0	23.2	18.1
United States and Canada	0.2	0.1	2.3	5.1	6.7	5.8
Latin America	2.2	1.5	2.8	3.9	6.3	8.3
Africa	18.4	13.2	8.1	7.4	8.8	10.4
Asia	60.8	65.9	64.0	58.6	55.0	57.4

Another way of presenting these population data is in the form of a graph. Note that the graph on page 27 makes more obvious the differences between numbers and thus makes comparisons easier. However, ease of comparison is traded for a loss in precision; the graph gives less specific numbers (reading along the vertical axis) than the table. A graph also requires more space to convey the same information as a table. The graph on page 27, were it to have included all of the time periods of the table, would have been very large.

The more detailed the data and their arrangement, the more historical information that can be displayed and the more intricate the comparisons that can be made. The table on pages 28–29 lists the percentage of the total vote and the number of deputies elected to the German parliament by each of the major political parties in each election from 1919 to 1933. (Note that in the parliamentary system, elections do not come at regular intervals.)

This table allows you to follow the changing fortunes of each political party. A wealth of information on German political history is contained in these figures. Between the lines one can also find pieces of the social and economic history of Germany. To choose only two examples, the strength of the Communist and Social Democratic (Socialist) parties attests to the deep dissatisfaction of many German workers with the state of the economy during the period known as the Weimar Republic. Even more striking is the tremendous growth of the National Socialist (Nazi) party after 1930. It was this development that brought Adolf Hitler to power in 1933. Eventually the results of that event would reverberate around the world. A table is not just numbers.

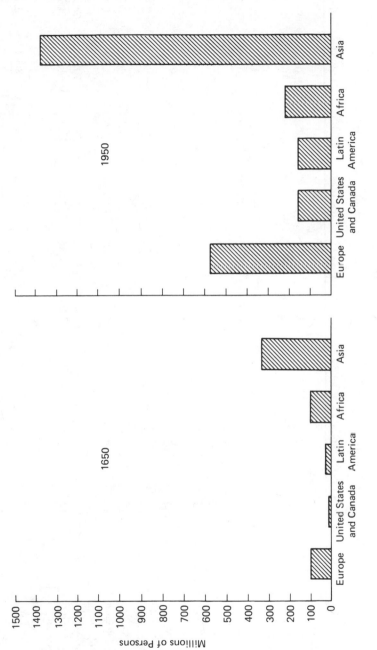

Estimated World Population

Reichstag Elections, 1919–1933 (Number of Deputies and Percentage of Total Votes*)

Party	1/19/19	6/6/20	5/4/24	12/7/24	5/20/28	9/14/30	7/31/32	11/6/32	3/5/33
Communist									
No. dep.	0	4	62	45	54	77	89	100	81
% vote		2.1%	12.6%	9.0%	10.6%	13.1%	14.6%	16.9%	12.3%
Social Democratic									
No. dep.			100	131	153	143	133	121	120
% vote			20.5%	26.0%	29.8%	24.5%	21.6%	20.4%	18.3%
Ind.									
No. dep.	22	84							
% vote	7.6%	17.9%							
Maj.									
No. dep.	165	102							
% vote	37.9%	21.6%							
Democratic									
No. dep.	75	39	28	32	25	20	4	2	5
% vote	18.6%	8.3%	5.7%	6.3%	4.9%	3.8%	1.0%	1.0%	0.8%
Centrum									
No. dep.	91	64	65	69	62	68	75	70	74
% vote	19.7%	13.6%	13.4%	13.6%	12.1%	11.8%	12.5%	11.9%	11.7%
Bavarian People's									
No. dep.	0	21	16	19	16	19	22	20	18
% vote		4.4%	3.2%	3.7%	3.0%	3.0%	3.2%	3.1%	2.7%

Economic									
No. dep.	4	4	10	17	23	23	2	1	0
% vote	0.9%	0.8%	2.4%	3.3%	4.5%	3.9%	0.4%	0.3%	0
German People's									
No. dep.	19	65	45	51	45	30	7	11	2
% vote	4.4%	13.9%	9.2%	10.1%	8.7%	4.5%	1.2%	1.9%	1.1%
National People's									
No. dep.	44	71	95	103	73	41	37	52	52
% vote	10.3%	14.9%	19.5%	20.5%	14.2%	7.0%	5.9%	8.8%	8.0%
National Socialist									
No. dep.	0	0	32	14	12	107	230	196	288
% vote	0	0	6.5%	3.0%	2.6%	18.3%	37.4%	33.1%	43.9%

*Under the electoral system provided for in the Weimar Constitution, each party received approximately one representative for every 60,000 popular votes cast for its candidates. Various small parties, not listed here, were underrepresented in the Reichstag.

From L. S. Stavrianos, *The World Since 1500: A Global History,* 4th ed. (Englewood Cliffs, N.J.: Prentice-Hall, 1991), p. 419.

How to Take Notes in Class

The first rule concerning note taking is simple: pay attention. Don't sleep, doodle, talk, stare out the window, or write a letter to a friend. Some lecturers are not exactly spellbinding or fully organized in what they say, but there is no point in going to class if you are not going to listen to the lecture.

Read the text before going to class or you may be taking notes on the material in the book. If everything the instructor says is new to you, you will spend so much time writing that you won't be able to get an understanding of the theme of the lecture. If you have obtained some basic information from outside readings, you will be able to concentrate on noting points in the lecture that are new or different.

An instructor is most likely to prepare exam questions from material that he or she considers most important. It is therefore essential in preparing notes to determine which points in the lecture are given most prominent attention. Some instructors are very open about their preferences and clearly emphasize certain points, often writing them on the blackboard. Never fail to note something that the instructor indicates is important. Other instructors are less explicit about their biases and values, and you will have to try to figure them out. Listen closely, and make note of those interpretations and generalizations that seem to be stressed, especially when they differ from the approach in the text. You should not feel obliged to parrot your instructor's interpretations in an exam, but ignorance of them will work against you.

Your notes should be written legibly and headed by the date and subject of the lecture. They should reflect a general outline of the material covered, with emphasis on major interpretations and important facts not covered by the text. It is often best to write on every other line and to leave a large margin on at least one side of the page. This will allow you to add material later and to underline your notes and write marginal comments without cluttering the page.

If possible, reread your notes later in the day on which they were written. If your handwriting is poor or your notes are disorganized, it is best to rewrite them. Check the spelling and definitions of any unfamiliar words, and be sure that the notes are coherent. Remember, your notes are an important source of information in your studies, and if they don't make sense, you won't either.

To illustrate some of the essentials of good note taking, here are portions of two sets of class notes taken from the same lecture. The first example illustrates many of the common errors of note takers, and the second is an example of a well-written set of notes. The subject of the lecture was early European contact with Africa.

Example of Poor Note Taking

Colonization of Africa—People were afraid to sail out. Afraid of sea monsters. But they liked the stories about gold in Africa. The Portuguese King Henry sailed south to find the gold mines and built a fort at Elmina.

England and France want to trade with Africa. They begin trading. Competing with Portugal. These countries got into wars. They wanted to control Africa.

China had spices. They traded with Cairo and Venice. The Asians wanted gold, but the Islams stopped all trade. They fought wars about religion for hundreds of years. Fought over Jerusalem. The Pope called for a crusade. This was in the Middle Ages.

Spices came from Asia. In Europe they were valuable because the kings used them to become rich. They also ate them.

The Portuguese wanted to explore Africa and make a way to India. Their boats couldn't get around until Bartholomew Diaz discovered the Cape of Good Hope in 1487.

Most of all, the Portuguese wanted slaves. They shipped them back from Africa. Columbus took them after he discovered America (1492). The Pope made a line in the Atlantic Ocean so the Catholics wouldn't fight. The colonies needed slaves. They sent 15 million from 1502 to the 19th century. Slaves did the hard work. They got free later after the Civil War.

Immigrants go to Africa from Europe but they don't like the hot weather and they catch diseases. The Dutch set up their own country at the Cape. Then the English conquer them.

Example of Good Note Taking

Early European Contact with Africa History 200
10/22/94

I. Why Did Europeans Come to Africa?
   A. Desire for gold
      1. Medieval legends about gold in Africa.

2. Prince Henry (Portuguese navigator) sent men down coast of Africa to find source of gold. (Also to gain direct access to gold trade controlled by Muslims.)
3. Portuguese built forts along the coast. Their ships carried gold and ivory back to Portugal (16th century).
4. Then the other European states came (England, Holland, France, Spain) to set up their own trading posts.
5. Competed with each other for African trade. (Will talk about rivalry next week.)

B. Wanted to trade with Asia and weaken the Muslims
(The Muslims had created a large empire based on the religion of Islam.)
1. Religious conflict between Christianity and Islam. Fought a religious war in the 11th–12th centuries—the Crusades.
2. The Muslims had expanded their empire when Europe was weak. In 15th century they controlled North Africa and they dominated trade in the Mediterranean. They controlled the spices coming from Asia, which were in great demand in Europe. In Europe they were used to preserve meat. So valuable, sometimes used as money.
3. Portugal and Spain were ruled by Catholic monarchs. Very religious. The Catholic monarchs wanted to force the Muslims out of Europe. (They still held part of Spain.) Wanted to convert them to Christianity.
4. The Muslims controlled North Africa and Mediterranean trade. If the Portuguese and Spanish could sail to the Indian Ocean directly, they could get goods from China and the Muslims couldn't stop them. The way to Asia was the sea route around Africa.

(margin: I M P O R T A N T)

C. The Europeans wanted slaves
1. When the Portuguese explored West Africa (15th century), they sent back the first slaves (around 1440).
2. The Spanish conquered the New World (Mexico, Peru, etc.). (Columbus had made several trips for Queen Isabella I of Spain.)
3. In America (the name for the New World), they needed slaves. Most slaves were sent to America.
4. Native Americans died from diseases of white men. They were also killed in the wars. There was nobody to run the mines (gold and silver).

5. Sugar plantations of the Caribbean (and Brazil) needed labor. Cotton plantations in the south of U.S. also. It was hard work and nobody wanted to do it.

6. 15 million (maybe as many as 40 million) slaves were brought to work the plantations starting in 1502 until mid-19th century.

II. Colonization
  A. Immigration (why white people didn't come)
    1. They couldn't take the climate.
    2. There were a lot of tropical diseases.
    3. The Europeans didn't want to live in Africa, only run it.
    4. Only the Dutch settlers came. They set up the Boer states in South Africa. After them came British settlers.
    5. Some French settled in Algeria.
    6. Some English also moved to Rhodesia.
  B. Dividing Africa
    1. Whites began exploring into the interior. (Will discuss exploration next week.)

Copying notes during a lecture is difficult, and even a good set of notes can be greatly improved by being rewritten. Following is a rewriting of these notes. Note how much clearer everything becomes.

Rewritten Good Notes

Early European Contact with Africa   History 200
                                                       10/22/94

I. What Drew Europeans to Africa?
    A. Gold
        There were medieval legends that there was a lot of gold in West Africa. Access to the gold was controlled by non-Christian powers (Muslims—believers in Islamic religion). Tales of gold lured the Portuguese (led by Prince Henry) to explore the coast of West Africa in the late 15th century. By the 16th century, the Portuguese had built several trading posts and forts along the West African coast and were bringing back gold, ivory, and pepper.
        By the 17th century, English, Dutch, French, and Spanish ships challenged the Portuguese trading monopoly and set up their own trading posts. This was the beginning of rivalry between European countries over the wealth of Africa.

B. Desire to weaken the power of the Islamic Empire (Muslims)
and expand trade with Asia

Conflict between Christianity and Islam was an old religious
conflict (the Crusades as an example in 11th and 12th
centuries). The Muslims controlled North Africa and the
Mediterranean. They also controlled the spice trade from Asia.
Spices were important in Europe because they were the only
known way to preserve meat.

The Catholic states of Portugal and Spain wanted to fight
with the Muslims. They wanted to drive them out of Spain
and challenge the large Muslim empire in Africa, the Middle
East, and Asia. They hoped to convert them to Christianity.
*The Muslims were strong in North Africa, but if European
powers could discover a way around Africa into the Indian
Ocean, they could outflank the Muslims and obtain direct
access to the trade with India and Asia.*

C. Slaves

Portuguese trading posts in Africa had sent a small number
of slaves to Europe starting in the late 15th century. With the
discovery and conquest of America at the turn of the 16th
century, a new and larger slave trade began to European
colonies in the New World (America).

The native Americans died (they were killed in war and by
European diseases in great numbers). There was a shortage of
labor. In the 17th and 18th centuries, large sugar plantations
were set up in the Caribbean and Brazil and cotton plantations
in the southern United States. *The need for laborers to do the
hard agricultural work led to the importing of millions of
slaves from Africa.* Somewhere between 15 and 40 million
Africans were sent to America as slaves between 1502 and the
mid-19th century. This slave trade made Africa valuable to the
European powers.

II. The Colonization of Africa

A. Immigration

Because of the unsatisfactory climate and tropical diseases,
there was no major European immigration to Africa. The only
significant white colony was set up in South Africa by the
Boers (Dutch) and later the English. There were smaller
European settlements in Rhodesia (English) and Algeria
(French).

　　B.　Dividing up the continent
　　　　1.　Exploration

If you reread the poor notes now, you can easily see how little of the lecture material is recorded in them and how confusing and even erroneous a picture you get from them. What is there about the poor notes that makes them inferior?

First, they are not organized. They do not even record the title of the lecture, the course number, or the date. If these notes get out of order, they will be useless. In fact, they are almost useless anyway. They are nothing more than a series of sentences about gold, trade, spices, Portugal, and slaves. The sentences are not in any particular order, and they do not say anything important. Even the factual information does not cover the major points of the lecture. Instead, it is peripheral information about sea monsters, China, Jerusalem, Bartholomew Diaz, and Columbus, most of which the good note taker wisely omitted. By paying too much attention to trivial points, moreover, the poor note taker missed or did not have time to record the principal theme of the lecture—the relationship between European-Asian trade and the religious struggle between Islam and Christianity. The poor note taker also missed another major point— the connection between the enslavement of Africans and the need for plantation labor in the New World. Without these two points, this student cannot write a good exam on this subject.

The good notes, on the other hand, follow the organization of the lecture and touch upon the major points made in class. The notes make sense and can serve as the basis for reviewing the content of the lecture when studying for exams.

These notes are not crowded, but well spaced so that material and emphasis can be added later if necessary. They also have a wide margin for extra comments and the marking of important passages. (Note the emphasis on B.4. and C.5.) The instructor had emphasized these points in class, and by making special note of them, the good student will be sure to master them.

The rewritten version, which eliminates certain unimportant or repetitious phrases and smoothes the language into connected sentences, is even better as a study guide. The greatest value of rewriting, however, is that by re-creating the lecture material in essay form, it becomes part of the note taker's own thinking. The mental effort that goes into revising lecture notes serves to impress the material and its meaning upon the mind. This makes it much easier to review the material at exam time.

How to Take Notes on Slides and Films

Some instructors present slide lectures or show films or videotapes. Note taking in these instances involves special problems. If a lecture is accompanied by slides, you will need to include in your notes information as to what the slides illustrated (for example, the Pyramid of Cheops, the novels of Willa Cather, the assassination of John F. Kennedy, the dances of Martha Graham) and anything of importance your instructor said about the slides.

Taking notes on films or videotapes presents some unusual problems. The lighting may be dim. The greatest problem may be the film itself. In our culture, films are a medium of entertainment rather than education. Your natural response will be to sit back and relax your mind. You must fight this response and learn to probe a film as you would a lecture. If a film is essentially factual (*Walled Cities of the Middle Ages*), note the major facts and interpretations as you would in a lecture. If a film is dramatic rather than documentary (*Ivan the Terrible, Citizen Kane*), examine the emotional message and artistic content as well as any historical facts it describes (or claims to describe). As with the author of a book, you need to ask: what is the movie director trying to say, and what dramatic and technical devices does he or she use to say it? Your notes should record important narration and dialogue that illustrate the theme of the film. More important, you will need to take note of pictorial elements (camera angle, sets, lighting, gestures and movements, facial expressions) because the core of a dramatic film and its impact are essentially visual. It takes practice to learn to take notes on slides and films. It will be worth the effort because photographs, films, and videotapes are used increasingly in history courses.

Class Participation

Many instructors encourage class participation, and some base a portion of the grade on it. Here are a few pointers for improving your ability to participate in class discussions.

1. Be familiar with the subject under discussion.
2. If a point is made that disagrees with your understanding, or if something in the lecture or discussion is confusing, formulate a clear question or statement in your mind.
3. If you don't get a chance to be recognized in class, bring up your question with the teacher when the session is over.
4. Teachers are not impressed with students who like to hear themselves talk or who ask careless questions, but if you are inter-

ested in the subject and have thought about what you want to say, never hesitate to speak up.

Giving a Formal Class Talk

If a course involves an oral presentation in class, you must learn something about this type of assignment. Eloquence and effectiveness in public speaking cannot be mastered in a week or two, but you can make a start by taking such an assignment seriously and adequately preparing yourself for it. Reading from a prepared text is often the safest procedure, but this can lead to a dull presentation. If you speak from notes, you will have to be fully familiar with your subject and pay more attention to getting your points across. Nevertheless, this kind of presentation will probably be livelier and more enjoyable for the class. You should prepare your talk outline as you would that of a short paper. (See Chapter 3, the section on "Short Papers."). Be sure that you cover all the important points and that you present them in a logical manner. A dry run before a relative, friend, or roommate is recommended. Be sure that you exhibit a knowledge of your subject because this is most likely to determine your grade. Effective public speaking is one of the most important tools of success in many fields of work, and giving a talk in class is a good opportunity to develop your skills in this area.

chapter **3**

How to Study for and Take an Exam, and How to Write a Book Review or Short Paper

Exams: How to Study for Them

When a test is announced, be sure to find out what kind of an exam it will be: essay, short answer, multiple choice, and so forth. Determine what topics will be covered and what portions of the reading material and lectures deal with the topics. If you have not done all of the necessary reading, do so immediately and record the important facts and interpretations as indicated in Chapter 2 in the section on "How to Read a History Assignment." If you have missed any lectures, obtain a copy of the notes from someone who knows the rules of good note taking. Now gather together all the materials to be covered in the exam. Reread the parts of the texts that you underlined (or otherwise noted) as being important. Reread *all* of the relevant lecture notes, paying special attention to any points emphasized by the instructor. Sometimes it helps to do your rereading aloud.

If the test is to be an essay exam, compose sample questions based upon the important topics and themes contained in the readings and lectures. (Many textbooks contain sample exam questions or topics for discussion at the end of each chapter.) If you do not know how to answer any portion of the sample question, go over your study materials again and look for the information needed. If you are preparing for an objective exam—that is, one requiring short answers—you must pay special attention to the important facts (persons, places, events, changes) in your study materials. You must be precise in order to get credit for your answer. Make a list of the outstanding people, events, and historical developments, and be sure that you can adequately identify them and explain their importance. (Again, your text may help you by providing sample short-answer questions.)

Take the time you need to prepare adequately. If tests make you nervous, the best medicine is to go into the exam confident that you know the material. Keep on studying until you have mastered your sample questions and until the material to be covered makes sense to you.

Taking Essay Exams

Even if you have prepared properly for an essay exam, your problems are not over. You must stay calm enough to remember what you studied, you must understand the questions, you must answer them directly and fully, and you must not run out of time. None of this is easy, but here are a few pointers to follow until you gain the experience to overcome these problems.

1. When you are given the exam, don't panic. Read the entire exam slowly, including all of the instructions. Gauge the amount of time you will need to answer each question. Then choose the question you know most about to answer first.
2. Don't write the first thing that comes to your mind. Read the question slowly, and be sure you understand it.
3. Determine how you will answer the question and the central points you wish to make.
4. Write these central points or even a full outline in the margin of the exam booklet, and as you compose each sentence of your answer, make sure that it relates to one of these points.
5. Your answer must follow the question. Be as specific or general, as concrete or reflective, as the question suggests. Never allow your answer to wander away from the focus of the question. If the question asks you to "describe" or "trace" or "compare" or "explain," be sure that that is what you do.

6. Don't repeat yourself. Each sentence should add new material or advance a line of argument.

7. Where necessary, refer to the facts that support the points you are making. You must also give evidence that you have thought about the question in broad terms. The mere relation of a series of facts will rarely earn you a high grade.

8. Toward the end of your answer, you may wish to include your own opinion. This is fine, even desirable, but be sure that your answer as a whole supports this opinion.

9. Always reread and correct an answer after it is finished. The pressure of an exam can often cause you to write sentences that are not clear.

10. Write legibly, or your grader will be in no mood to give you the benefit of any doubts.

11. Don't write cute or plaintive notes on the exam. They seldom raise a grade and may prejudice the grader against you.

A well-written essay answer is a combination of (1) adequate knowledge of the subject, (2) clear thinking about the points to be covered, (3) well-structured sentences, and (4) complete understanding of the question. Following are two answers to a sample essay question on modern Chinese history. The first answer is very well written and deals successfully with the four requirements listed. The second answer is very poor and meets none of these requirements.

Question: Discuss the origins of the Chinese Civil War of 1945–1949. How did the differing political programs of the two contenders affect the outcome of that conflict?

Good Answer

The origins of the 1945–1949 Civil War can be traced back to the rise of Chinese nationalism in the late nineteenth century. Out of the confusion of the Warlord period that followed the overthrow of the Manchu dynasty in 1911, two powerful nationalist movements arose—one reformist and the other revolutionary. The reformist movement was the Guo Mindang (Kuomintang), founded by Sun Zhongshan (Sun Yat-sen). It was based on a mixture of republican, Christian, and moderate socialist ideals and inspired by opposition to foreign domination. The revolutionary movement was that of the Chinese Communist Party (CCP), founded in 1921, whose goal was a communist society but whose immediate program was to organize the working class to protect its interests and to work for the removal of foreign "imperialist" control.

Although these two movements shared certain immediate goals (suppression of the Warlords and resistance to foreign influence), they eventually fell out over such questions as land reform, relations with the Soviet Union, the role of the working class, and the internal structure of the Guo Mindang (Kuomintang). [The CCP operated within the framework of the more powerful Guo Mindang (Kuomintang) during the 1920s.]

By the 1930s, when Jiang Jieshi (Chiang Kai-shek) succeeded Sun, the CCP was forced out of the Guo Mindang (Kuomintang). By that time the CCP had turned to a program of peasant revolution inspired by Mao Zedong (Mao Tse-tung). A four-year military struggle (1930–1934) between the two movements for control of the peasantry of Jiangxi (Kiangsi) Province ended in the defeat but not destruction of the CCP.

The Japanese invasion of Manchuria (1931) and central China (1936–1938) helped salvage the fortunes of the CCP. By carrying out an active guerrilla resistance against the Japanese, in contrast to the more passive role of the Guo Mindang (Kuomintang) which was saving its army for a future battle with the Communists, the CCP gained the leading position in the nationalist cause.

In the post-World War II period, the CCP's land reform program won strong peasant support, whereas the landlord-backed Guo Mindang (Kuomintang) was faced with runaway corruption and inflation, which eroded its middle-class following. The military struggle between 1945 and 1949 led to the defeat of the demoralized Guo Mindang (Kuomintang) army and the coming to power of the CCP.

Poor Answer

The Guo Mindang (Kuomintang) had a stronger army than the Communists, but the Communists won the civil war and took over the country. Their political program, communism, was liked by the peasants because they didn't own any land and paid high taxes.

China was based on the Confucian system, which was

very rigid and led to the Manchu dynasty being overthrown. The Chinese didn't like being dominated by foreigners, and Sun Zhongshan (Sun Yat-sen) founded the Guo Mindang (Kuomintang) to unite China. He believed in the Three People's Principles. At first he cooperated with the Chinese Communists, but later Jiang Jieshi (Chiang Kai-shek) tried to destroy communism because he was against it. Communism was not in favor of the wealthy people.

The Communists wanted a revolution of the peasants and gave them land. They also killed the landlords. Jiang Jieshi (Chiang Kai-shek) worried more about the Communists than about the Japanese invasion. The Japanese looked to conquer China and make it a part of their empire. Jiang Jieshi (Chiang Kai-shek) wanted to fight the Communists first.

After World War II the Chinese Communists attacked Manchuria and took over a lot of weapons. They fought the Guo Mindang (Kuomintang) army. The Guo Mindang (Kuomintang) army lost the battles, and Jiang Jieshi (Chiang Kai-shek) was chased to Taiwan, where he made a new government. The Communists set up their own country, and their capital was Beijing (Peking). That way the Communists won the Chinese Civil War.

Let's see the differences between the poor and the well-written essays in regard to each of the four requirements for a well-written answer.

1. *Adequate knowledge of the subject.* The poor answer fails to indicate adequate knowledge in several ways. It is too brief, omitting many important facts. It describes the political programs of the two contending parties in the most vague terms. It refers to the CCP only as the Chinese Communists, leaving the impression that they were a loose grouping of like-minded individuals rather than a strong, well-disciplined political organization. It does not even mention the name of the most famous leader of the CCP—Mao Zedong (Mao Tse-tung). Jiang Jieshi (Chiang Kai-shek), the leader of the Guo Mindang (Kuomintang), is mentioned, but there is no mention of his political program or beliefs, other than that he was opposed to communism. Another serious defect is the lack of chronology. The answer jumps back and forth between earlier and later periods, and no dates are given for major events.

The well-written answer illustrates a good knowledge of the subject matter. The origins, philosophies, leaders, and relationship of the two contending parties are clearly described. This answer brings in related issues such as nationalism, Warlords, guerrilla warfare against Japan, corruption, and inflation, thus indicating a broader knowledge of the historical context in which the Chinese Civil War developed. The chronology is very clear, with events proceeding in proper time sequence and with all major events identified by date.

2. *Clear thinking about the points to be covered.* The poor answer is not organized. Note that the paragraphs do not make separate points and that each succeeding paragraph does not further develop the theme of the essay. Paragraph one is a conclusion rather than an introduction. The second paragraph goes back to the founding of the Guo Mindang (Kuomintang) but, instead of discussing the origins of the hostility between it and the CCP, merely states that hostility came into existence. The third paragraph begins by introducing the CCP (though not by name). However, it does not expand on the CCP's programs and points of conflict with the Guo Mindang (Kuomintang), but instead abruptly changes the focus of events and the time frame by introducing the Japanese invasion of China, which the last sentence of the paragraph only vaguely relates to the question. The last paragraph, instead of drawing conclusions about the causes of the Communist victory in the Civil War, merely states that it occurred.

The well-written answer, on the other hand, uses each paragraph to make a separate important point, and each succeeding paragraph further develops the theme of the essay. Paragraph one sets out the political programs of the two groups and the historical context in which the movements originated. The second paragraph explains the beginning of the conflict in the 1920s. Paragraph three discusses that conflict in relation to the Chinese peasantry during the early 1930s. The fourth paragraph discusses the development of the conflict in relation to the Japanese invasion of the late 1930s. The final paragraph summarizes the effects of the conflicts and of postwar developments on the outcome of the Civil War.

3. *Well-structured sentences.* Many sentences in the poor answer are badly constructed either because they are awkward or because what they say adds nothing to the answer. Some of the awkward phrases are "the Communists won the Civil War and *took over* the country"; "communism was *liked by* the peasants"; "China was *based on* the Confucian system"; "communism was not *in favor of* the wealthy people"; "the Japanese *looked to* conquer China"; "the Communists *set up their own country.*" These phrases cause the sentences to be unclear, and they keep the student from getting his or her point across. The other major

defect in sentence structure is repetitious or irrelevant sentences and phrases. These are "Jiang Jieshi (Chiang Kai-shek) tried to destroy communism *because he was against it*"; "they *fought the Guo Mindang (Kuomintang) army*"; "that way *the Communists won the Chinese Civil War.*" The sentences of the well-written answer, on the other hand, are clear, and each adds new material to the essay.

4. *Complete understanding of the question.* The poor answer does not deal with the central issue of the question—the political programs of the Guo Mindang (Kuomintang) and the CCP. It notes that the Guo Mindang (Kuomintang) was founded on the Three People's Principles, but it does not explain what these were. Of the CCP, it says that there was a belief in communism (which is obvious) and peasant revolution (which is vague). These are the only references to political programs in the entire answer! It is obvious that the writer of this answer failed to understand that the central focus of the question was on political philosophy.

The well-written answer is directed to the central issue of political programs and begins on that very point. The remainder of the answer makes clear the relationship of political programs to the origins and course of the Chinese Civil War as called for in the first sentence of the question.

Here is another good answer to an essay question. Note how it meets the four requirements set out above.

Question: Describe Russian expansion across Siberia. What factors facilitated this expansion? How did it compare with the expansion of the United States across North America?

Good Answer

Russian expansion to the east began in the sixteenth century from the area around Moscow, which had become the center of a powerful state under Ivan the Terrible (1533–1584). Eastern expansion was spearheaded by the Cossacks, who were in most instances former peasants who had fled to the frontiers of the Russian state to avoid serfdom. There they became shepherds, hunters, and expert horsemen. Some joined robber bands and preyed on commerce. Eventually they took up arms in service to the Russian nobility and fought against the Siberian Tatars, Moslem peoples who raided Russia from across the Ural Mountains. In a series of wars against the Tatars, Cossack forces fought and marched across northern Eurasia, covering a distance even greater than that across the United States, and reached the Pacific Ocean before the middle of the seventeenth century.

This vast territory was conquered in a brief period of time because of several favorable conditions. In a wide band of territory stretching eastward, the climate was similar to that of European Russia. Within this forested zone there were no major natural obstacles. The mountains were low and the rivers navigable. The native population was small and no powerful tribes existed. None had armaments equal to those of the Cossacks.

There are several similarities between Russian and United States continental expansion. The great extent of the two expansions is similar, as is the influence of the frontier experience on both cultures. Continental expansion in both cases engulfed (and often destroyed) weaker native peoples and incorporated their lands into the expanding nation rather than holding them as colonies. In both cases an important economic incentive was the fur trade and the ability of trappers to use the extensive river systems to send their pelts to market.

In some respects, however, the expansionist experiences were different. The Russian advance was much more rapid than the American. Cossacks began to push eastward about the same time (late sixteenth century) as the first English settlers came to America. By the mid-seventeenth century, however, the Russians had reached the Pacific Ocean while the settlers in North America had yet to cross the

Appalachian Mountains. Although the Russian advance was swift, settlement of the land was sparse compared with the slower American expansion. In 1763, all across the newly conquered expanse of Siberia there were only 400,000 Russians. At about the same date, the much smaller territory of the thirteen English colonies in North America contained about 1.7 million settlers.

The two expansions were similar in scope and in the nature of the native forces encountered. They were, however, different in content. Siberia is to this day a rather backward, isolated, and thinly populated region of Russia, whereas the lands that lie beyond the early eastern settlements of the United States today hold the greater part of the population and economic resources of the nation.

Objective Exams

Objective exams call for short factual answers. The questions may be multiple-choice, true-false, or definitions and identifications. If a simple choice is called for, think carefully about the alternatives before choosing. Read the question very carefully and don't jump to conclusions. If definitions or identifications are called for, answer briefly and directly. If you know only part of an answer, put that down, but don't add unrelated material just to make your answer look more impressive. You will be wasting your time. Moreover, don't try to change the question into one that you *can* answer. You won't get credit for an answer to a question that was not asked.

Here are some sample exam questions.

Short Answer Question: What were the motives that caused European powers to explore Africa beginning in the late fifteenth century?

Incorrect Answer

They wanted to dominate Africa and get all the gold for themselves. Columbus wanted to take the slaves from Africa, but the Pope said it would start a war. But the war didn't start and the Europeans dominated Africa.

Correct Answer

> The wars between Christianity and Islam were an important factor. The Christian states wanted to weaken the hold of the Muslim religion in Africa and to convert the natives. They also hoped to break Muslim control of trade with Asia by finding a sea route around Africa.

Check these two answers against the example of good note taking on pages 31–35, and you will see why the second answer is satisfactory while the first is not.

Based on your reading of this book so far, answer the following objective-exam questions.

Identification Question: Progressive school of historical interpretation.

(Check your answer against the definition on page 12.)

True-False Question: The Japanese invasion of Manchuria in 1931 destroyed the Chinese Communist Party.

Multiple-Choice Question: The founder of the Kuomintang Party in China was:
a) Jiang Jieshi (Chiang Kai-shek)
b) Mao Zedong (Mao Tse-tung)
c) Ho Chi-minh
d) Song Meiling (Soong Mei-ling)
e) Sun Zhongshan (Sun Yat-sen)

(Check your answers against the good exam essay on pages 40–41.)

Take-home Exams

A take-home exam is usually a series of short essays. The construction of your answers should generally follow the procedure for writing a short paper. (See pages 52–53.) There are, however, a few specific guides to this type of assignment.

Prepare your answer by outlining those portions of the textbook or collateral readings that deal with the exam question. Then list the most important points covered in these sources—generally two to six for each question. Compose your answer by discussing each of these points in some logical order. As with all essays, it is best to have a central theme.

A problem that sometimes arises with take-home exams is plagiarism.

In such an exam, it is usually permissible to paraphrase the sources used in preparing your answer. Be sure, however, that you write in your own words. If you use sentences from a book in your answer, you are cheating, whether you mean to or not. Copying from a text or history work is unlikely to get you anywhere. Your instructor knows that experienced historians write quite differently from students, and passages taken from such a source will jump out of the page as your paper is being read. Most instructors penalize students severely for plagiarizing. (See Chapter 4, the section on "Avoiding Plagiarism.")

Book Reviews

A book review is an essay whose purpose is to comment on a particular work or a series of works bearing upon a single subject. The most important point to remember about a book review is that it is a *commentary*, not merely a summary. Unless your instructor specifically requests that you survey the contents, a book review should spend little time outlining the material covered by the author. The bulk of your report should be an evaluation of the way the author handled the subject, and a commentary on the book's contribution to your understanding of the issues discussed. Your review should discuss the author's theme and point of view, as well as your reaction to them; evaluate the author's methodology (rules for organizing evidence); discuss the author's values and biases; and draw conclusions as to how well the author's point comes across.

It may be necessary to refer to specific portions of the book to illustrate your statements and conclusions, but it is generally not advisable to quote from it. If you know something of the author's other works, it is appropriate for you to make these a part of your critical evaluation. When you are reviewing several works on a common subject, it is also appropriate to devote a portion of your paper to a comparison of their use of evidence, their success in supporting their themes, and their respective conclusions.

The form of a book review is similar to that of any essay. You should begin by making a list of points you wish to make. If more than two or three works are involved, do not discuss each one separately. Choose aspects of the subject that are general enough to cover all of them, and then compare the books from those particular perspectives. There is no need to give an accounting of the contents of each book.

Once your list of central points has been compiled, you should take each one as the focus of a different section of your review. (Don't try to make more points than can be accomplished in a brief book review. It is better to make a few points well than many points poorly.) Each section of your review should explain the point, support it with your own arguments and with brief examples from the book(s) under review, and then draw conclusions as to the meaning and importance of the point.

Because a book review is generally brief, come to the point directly and confine yourself to a small number of supporting examples. It should be clear to the instructor not only that you have read the book(s) but also that you have thought about what you have read and have used your own experience and critical faculties in formulating your comments.

To help you to see these rules and suggestions in practice, here is an example of a book review of the work you are now reading.

> John Q. Student
>
> History 100
>
> October 14, 1994

Book Review of:

Jules R. Benjamin

A Student's Guide to History

St. Martin's Press, 6th ed., 1994

Benjamin's purpose, as stated in the preface, is to introduce students to the subject of history and to provide them with study and research skills. The author includes sections on such matters as "What History Can Tell You," "How to Read a History Assignment," "Avoiding Plagiarism," and "Organizing a Bibliography." These subjects and others are presented clearly and succinctly, often with examples. It does seem, however, that Benjamin has only the beginning student in mind and thus explains some matters (such as how to answer an objective-exam question) that seem to be matters of common sense.

The most valuable sections of the book are those

entitled: "A Brief Journey into the Past" and "How to
Research Your Family History." In "A Brief Journey . . . ."
Benjamin makes clear how history surrounds us if we only
know how to look for it. The section on family history is
very useful to anyone conducting that kind of research.
Nevertheless, the author could have given greater
attention to this topic, despite the need to cover many
other subjects.

Benjamin's point of view is consistently student
oriented, attempting to fill study and research needs
while still paying some attention to history as an
intellectual field. Overall, the book is clearly of the
"how to" variety. The discussion of the philosophy of
history is very brief, and only passing mention is made of
the field of historiography.

Perhaps the most successful part of the book is the
long appendix: "Basic Reference Sources for History Study
and Research." Here the author lists dozens of different
kinds of reference works (dictionaries, encyclopedias,
atlases, biography collections, periodical guides) and
page after page of bibliographies on specialized periods,
areas, or topics in history. The section devoted to
bibliographies on "Asian Immigrant and Ethnic History" was
very helpful in finding books for a paper on "The Chinese
in Nineteenth-Century San Francisco." The list of sources
in the appendix is very broad but seems to be most
complete in Benjamin's own area of interest, which,
according to the Directory of American Scholars, is in
modern United States history.

All in all, Benjamin has created a useful and
interesting guide for history students. It enables the

student to acquire a better understanding of the purpose
of a history course and to get more out of it by using the
skills discussed in A Student's Guide to History.

Here is another example of a book review, this time one written by a professional historian. This is the way it appeared in the book review section of a history journal.[1]

An Economic History of Argentina in the Twentieth Century. By Laura Randall. New York, Columbia University Press, 1978. pp. 323. $21.90

Reviewed by Jonathan C. Brown
Lecturer in History
University of California, Los Angeles

Of the national economies of Latin America, that of Argentina is one of the more thoroughly researched. So why another book on the twentieth century Argentine economy? Laura Randall's volume is not just another survey but a detailed exposition of the economic policies of the national government and their impact on the development process. Her analysis shows how the government's policies in banking, agriculture, manufacturing, petroleum, and transport gradually have weaned the Argentine economy from its turn-of-the-century domination by British and foreign interests.

Randall's thesis is straightforward. Shifts in Argentina's political control provoked change in the nation's economic structure. Central to her argument is the theory of "alternate profit opportunities," which explains the actions of Argentine investors according to their expectations of future profits. Randall concludes that the behavior of businessmen in Argentina often depended upon who was president. She argues that political policies in a number of areas have mitigated the effect of international determinants on Argentine economic growth. For instance, the Banco de la Nación determines the supply of money and allocates credit according to government dictates. Thus, the government can and does use its leverage to influence the timing, size, and distribution of economic growth nationwide. This may not assure an even growth pattern, for political policies consistently have favored the province of Buenos Aires over the western and northern provinces of the country.

Growth of Argentina's domestic manufacturing since World War I provides an apt case study of this increasing governmental direction of the economy. Desiring greater economic autarchy, Argentine policymakers have instituted a series of protective tariffs, tax incentives, and preferential credit arrangements

[1]*Business History Review*, vol. 53, no. 1, Spring, 1979, pp. 144–145. Reprinted by permission of the Harvard Business School.

that guaranteed high profits to domestic industrialists. Although President Juan Perón cannot be credited with originating the idea of industrial self-sufficiency, his economic planners in particular vigorously stimulated import-substitution industrialization. Thus, designated "national interest" industries grew three times faster than Argentine manufacturing as a whole between 1950 and 1955.

Randall's analysis goes to the pith of an important issue: has Argentine economic development in this century been dependent upon foreign factors? She argues that it has not! She cites the decreasing size of foreign investment relative to total investment (from 17 per cent in the 1920s to 2 per cent recently) and the declining importance of exports to total GDP (from 25 per cent in the 1920s to 6 per cent in the 1970s). As further evidence, Randall measures the determinants of economic output in this century. Using regression equations and correlation coefficients, she finds that the variables of the presidency, fiscal policy, and government spending were more important to economic performance. "Foreign factors" such as export earnings, import expenditures, and foreign exchange proved quantitatively less significant.

Scholars will be hard pressed to ignore this important contribution to the understanding of Argentina's economic development. The arguments are well documented and clearly presented. In addition, Randall's analysis and statistical measures of the Argentine economy may serve as a model for the assessment of the political economies of other Latin American countries as well.

Short Papers

A short paper (about five to ten pages) is not truly a research project. It is more of a report or essay on a particular topic based on the reading of a half-dozen or so sources. A take-home essay exam is even shorter but is organized in essentially the same way. Many of the aspects of short papers and take-home essay exams, however, are themselves similar to the preparation of a longer research paper. (For the preparation of a research paper see chapters four and five.)

A short paper should combine a brief review of the works read in preparation for the paper with a longer development of a particular theme. The theme is the central focus of the paper, and all your references, arguments, and conclusions should be related to it. (For the development of a theme, see pages 81–82.)

Before writing your paper, you should first go through the books you have read on the subject and list the most important factual or interpretive points that you wish to use in support of your theme. You can then arrange these points in some logical progression and write a paragraph or two explaining each point and showing its connection to and support of your general theme. These paragraphs (approximately three to six pages) are the core of your text. This core should be preceded by a one- or two-page introduction, the purpose of which is to explain your theme to the reader. The core should be followed by a one- or two-page conclusion, the purpose of which is to draw together and summarize the arguments that support your theme and explain the importance of the theme and its relationship to other important issues. (For more on organizing a paper, see pages 82–83.)

When the rough draft is finished, revise any section that is poorly written, that fails to support your theme, or that wanders into other subjects. Check for spelling and grammar. Read it aloud, and, keeping your reader in mind, make sure your theme comes across clearly and forcefully.

The form of a short paper can vary greatly, and you should be guided by your instructor's suggestions. If footnotes are required, one or two per page usually are sufficient, unless you are advised otherwise. In a short paper, footnote only direct quotations and especially controversial statements. (For rules regarding footnotes, see pages 97–102.) In general, a short paper should not contain lengthy quotations. (For rules regarding quotations, see pages 103–104.) Regardless of its size, however, a short paper should contain a bibliography. (For rules concerning bibliographies, see pages 104–106.) A short paper or take-home essay should be carefully and neatly written. If possible, it should be typed double-spaced, with adequate margins on all sides. (For typing form, see page 106–107.)

A common assignment for a short paper is the "thematic essay." Although you may be given a choice (as with a longer research paper), the topic of a thematic essay is usually assigned. The topic is an important historical issue such as the effects of the French Revolution or the causes of the American Civil War. These issues commonly take the form of such questions as "Was American entry into World War I necessary?" and "Was the New Deal revolutionary or conservative?" The books or readings that form the basis of your research for this paper also are usually assigned. These works contain several selections—written from different points of view or using different historical evidence or methods—all of which deal with the central issue or question. When preparing a thematic essay, it is important to have the central historical issue clear in your mind and to be able to describe the major arguments and evidence of each selection in regard to that issue.

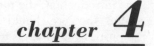
How to Research
a History Topic

In basic history courses, you may be called upon to do historical research. If you take advanced courses, you certainly will be called upon to do research papers. Whether you are preparing a short essay or book review or a long class presentation or term paper, you will need to know how to gather all the necessary materials and how to organize and analyze your information. This chapter will survey sources of historical information and will explain how to use these sources most profitably. The chapter also includes sections on how to record information and how to organize your notes.

Selecting a Topic

If you are given a choice of research topics, choose carefully. Doing research on a subject that does not interest you can be very boring. Try to select a topic about which you are genuinely curious. No matter what subject, person, or event you are interested in, it has a history. Every subject can be studied backward in time because every event was caused by events that preceded it. A history research project can be made out of almost anything. Perhaps in the neighborhood where you grew up there was a very old building and you had always wondered about when it was built and what it was used for. Finding out what the neighborhood was like when that building was new can be an exciting search.

An ideal topic is not only one about which you are curious but one about which you already know something. Perhaps you read a book about Socrates and want to know more about why he was condemned to death; or perhaps you saw a movie about the Depression and want to know what it was like to live through it. Instructors are eager to help students who show a real interest in a topic. Your instructor can assist you in selecting a subject related to your interests that also suits the particular course you are taking.

Formulating Your Topic

Once you have chosen a general topic (the Spanish conquest of the Aztec Empire, or the Reconstruction government of South Carolina), you should decide which specific aspect is most interesting to you, historically relevant, and most suitable to your limits of time and sources. You will not have time to properly develop a broad topic, and your sketchy treatment would not earn a satisfactory grade.

To pare down your topic to workable size, ask yourself what it is that you are most interested in finding out about. If your subject is the native Americans of the Plains, maybe you are most curious about the practice of magic by the Blackfoot nation or how the Cheyenne got the swift Arabian horses they rode. Be careful that the questions you ask are not too broad ("Why did the Roman Empire collapse?"), too narrow ("Who was the first person to sign the Declaration of Independence?"), or too unimportant ("Why are Ping-Pong tables green?").

If you know very little about your topic, you must learn more about it before you can narrow it successfully. If your general topic is the Mexican Revolution of 1910, check a brief outline history of the subject in a good historical dictionary or encyclopedia (for example, the *Encyclopaedia Britannica* or the *Encyclopedia of Latin America*). The description of the Mexican Revolution in these works will likely mention its principal leaders—Francisco Madero, Pancho Villa, Emiliano Zapata, and Venustiano Carranza. Perhaps your interest will now be triggered by the recollection of stories concerning Villa's daring raid on a United States border town (Columbus, New Mexico) in 1916 and how the U.S. Army under General Pershing marched into Mexico to capture him—but never did. Or perhaps you have seen the Hollywood movie *Viva Zapata*, which tells the story (not necessarily accurately) of the peasant leader Emiliano Zapata and his fight to preserve the lands of the Indian villages in his native state of Morelos. If you have ever seen photographs of Zapata (and they were popular in poster form among college students in the 1960s), you know his piercing eyes and look of determination. If your interest in the Mexican Revolution is now focusing on Villa or Zapata, you should next turn to a biographical dictionary. Here you will discover that Villa's real name was Doroteo Arango and that he was a cattle thief as well as a brilliant military commander. Zapata, you will learn, led a peasant guerrilla army whose aim was to recapture the land taken from its villages by owners of expanding sugar plantations. To flesh out a paper on Villa's military career or Zapata's land reform program (some elements of which Mexican peasants are still struggling for today), turn to the subject bibliographies in Appendix A of this book or to the reference section of your library. Subject bibliographies will lead you to individual historical works on the Mexican Revolution, and from the book and article titles (and the descriptions of their contents if they are annotated) you will be able to determine those which may contain information on the topic you are considering.

If learning about a topic does not help you to narrow it, try formulating a question that you would like your research to answer. For example, were Canadian frontier communities similar to those of the United States in the nineteenth century? This topic can be narrowed by choosing one or two aspects of such communities to compare—for instance, housing, government, economic function, or forms of entertainment. You could also narrow your topic geographically (e.g., prairie towns) or chronologically (e.g., communities founded in the 1850s). Formulating a question will also help you to confine your research to works that help to answer the question.

After (1) conducting preliminary research to help you decide what part of your topic interests you most, (2) narrowing it to manageable size, and (3) formulating a question or theme to direct your research, you will be ready to seek out sources of information on your final topic. The reference works listed in Appendix A will help you create a list of books, articles, and other relevant sources. If these works lead you to specific sources (e.g., the title of a book or the volume of a periodical), the next step is to see whether your school library has them. You will also want to know of any other books, articles, and so on that your library possesses on your topic. To find these sources, you will first have to learn how to conduct library research.

Finding Information on Your Topic in Your School Library

The best way to uncover materials in your school library that relate to your topic is to approach the task with certain *key words* in mind. Key words, in most cases, are the nouns that appear in the tentative formulation of your topic. If your subject is the partitioning of India, your key word is *India*. If it is the use of the submarine in World War I, you have two key words—*submarine* and *World War I*. These are the words that you will look up in the library catalogs and reference books.

A college library can be intimidating if you do not know how it is organized. There are three principal pathways through the library's collection of books, journals, magazines, newspapers, and documents: (1) the card catalog, (2) the computerized catalog, and (3) the collection of reference books. Each of these pathways leads you to information on your topic. You will need to learn how to use each of these research paths. Some of the advantages and problems of using each are described in the following sections.

The Card Catalog

Today, these long cabinets with drawer after drawer of 3″ × 5″ cards are usually referred to as the "old" card catalog. Before the era of computers, this was the principal avenue into the information contained in the library. Currently, almost all libraries have begun the long process of transferring the information on these cards onto computers. Your own library may not yet have a computerized "on-line" catalog, or it may have one that contains only recent acquisitions—that is, material that the library received since it installed its computer terminals. If so, you will need to include an examination of the old card catalog in your research effort. Other libraries have almost all of their holdings on computers. Your librarian can tell you whether it is best for you to begin your research in the *card* or the *on-line* catalog.

The card catalog is separated into three parts. One group of shelves contains cards organized alphabetically by *title*, another by *author*, and another by *subject*.[1]

Searching the Card Catalog by Title

If you already know the title of one of the books you are looking for or if your key word is a very specific one, then you can begin your search in the title section of the card catalog. Suppose your topic is Abraham

---

[1]Some large libraries also have separate card catalogs for special collections such as reference books, journals and magazines, newspapers, and microforms (information contained on microfilm, microfiche, and compact discs).

Lincoln's attitude toward slavery. *Lincoln* is one of your key words; by
following the alphabetical organization of the card catalog, you will come
to the drawer that holds cards for most of the books in the library whose
title contains the word *Lincoln*. When the title on a specific card indicates that the book may contain information on your topic, be sure to
copy down (on your own 3″ × 5″ card) all of the important information.
This information is located at the top of the card and includes the title of
the work, the author's name, and, in the top left corner, the "call number." The call number indicates the place on the library's shelves where
the work is located. Of course, you must spell your key word correctly. If
your topic is the philosophy of Mohandas *Gandhi* and you are looking
under *Ghandy*, you are in for a long day at the library. Be sure to check
the spelling of all key words in a good dictionary.

Correct spelling is also important if your key word is a place name. You
will not find books about Hawaii under *Howayi*. Even more troublesome
is the fact that over time the names of places change. Books about Persia
are now usually filed under its newer name, *Iran;* Belgian Congo under
Zaire; New Spain under *Mexico*. A good catalog will tell you of any newer
or older name by which a particular place is known. Geographical subdivisions can be a problem. Brittany is part of France, Honshu part of Japan,
Umbria part of Italy, Alberta part of Canada. The name of an important
subdivision may have its own place in the alphabetical listing of cards or it
may be listed with books about the larger area of which it is a part.
Geographical adjectives can present another difficulty with place names.
Some adjectives are part of the proper names of areas and should be listed
in their alphabetical order; others are not. North Dakota is a specific place
and will be found under "N" while northern California will be under "C."

Searching the Card Catalog by Author
This is the easiest path of all. If your key word is a person who wrote
books, whose writings, sayings, speeches, or other remarks have been
recorded in books, or about whom others have written books (biographies, for example), you merely check the alphabetical listing of Author
cards under the person's last name and then his or her first name (e.g.,
Washington, George). Again, be sure that the spelling is correct. The
spelling of foreign authors' names can be very tricky. A good biographical
dictionary can be helpful here. Again, when you find the author you are
looking for, copy down the full name, title, and call number.

Searching the Card Catalog by Subject
Unless your key word is the name of an important historical person or
place, or someone who wrote important works and about whom others

have written, the Subject card catalog is the place where you must begin your search. Here the search is more complex and is similar to looking things up in the yellow pages of the telephone book where car parts are not under "C" but under "A" for *Automotive Accessories* and toasters are under *Electrical Appliances* (or just *Appliances*). If you cannot find a subject heading in the catalog to match your key word, first check the spelling. Then think of a larger subject of which your key word is a part. For example, if your key word is *surgery* and you cannot find it under "S," it may be listed as a subheading under *Medicine*. It will probably appear there as "Medicine—Surgery." You might find railroads listed under *Transportation* and capital punishment under *Law*.

The example of a catalog card shown below indicates that a book entitled *A History of Surrealist Art* appears under the subject heading "Art - History - Modern." Note that you could also have found it by looking under *Surrealism*.

The subject card catalog is usually organized to help you find subdivisions of a subject. If you are looking up *Wilderness Campaign*, the card in that place may say "see Civil War" since that campaign was a series of battles in that war. At times you *will* find a group of cards, each with a book on your key word, but you will also find a card at the beginning or end of this group that says, for example, "see also Civil War—Battles." If your key word is *tariff*, together with the books on that subject may be a card that says "see also Trade." Unless you feel sure that the "see also" heading is too broad (that is, that it takes you to sources outside your topic), look at the cards under that heading also.

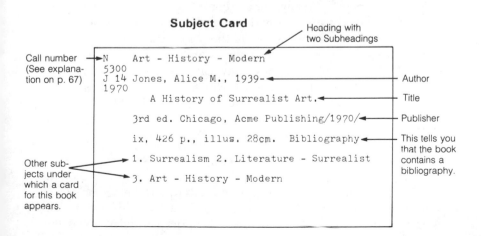

Subject Card

Heading with two Subheadings

Call number (See explanation on p. 67)

```
N      Art - History - Modern
5300
J 14  Jones, Alice M., 1939-          ← Author
1970
        A History of Surrealist Art.  ← Title

      3rd ed. Chicago, Acme Publishing/1970/  ← Publisher

      ix, 426 p., illus. 28cm.  Bibliography  ← This tells you
                                                 that the book
                                                 contains a
                                                 bibliography.
      1. Surrealism 2. Literature - Surrealist

      3. Art - History - Modern
```

Other subjects under which a card for this book appears.

THE PROBLEM OF SUBHEADINGS

Your ability to discover the place or places in the catalog that contain the books that focus directly on your topic can be greatly increased by learning to think in terms of subject divisions like the ones just discussed. (This same skill will be useful when you use the computerized on-line catalog.) The card catalog breaks down large subjects ("United States," "Economics," "Women's History," "Education") into a series of subheadings, moving from the most general to the most specific. Suppose your topic is labor support for the Perón Administration in Argentina. Your key words are *labor, Perón,* and *Argentina. Labor* is too broad a key word and will have to be broken down. *Argentina* is broad too, but note how the subject catalog helps you to arrive at the best subheading. Under *Argentina* in the subject catalog, you will come first to books about Argentina in general. After these will come the more specialized works, each group with its own subheading. It may look something like this: "Argentina—Economy," "Argentina— Foreign Relations," "Argentina—Politics," "Argentina—Travel Literature," and so forth. Some of these subheadings will be broken down even further. "Argentina—History" will be followed by "Argentina— History—to 1800." After that might come "Argentina—History—1800 to 1900" and after that "—1900 to Present." For your paper on Perón, you will want the section listing works that deal with Argentine history, 1900 to the present, since Perón was in power after 1940. If the history categories are not broken down any further and if none of the works under "1900 to Present" deal specifically with Perón, try the subheadings of "Argentina—Politics," "Argentina—Economy," and "Argentina—Labor." Finally, since Perón was an important figure about whom books have been written, the Title catalog, under *Perón, Juan Domingo* (his full name with the last name first), should list books written about him and will also contain any book by him, perhaps collections of his speeches. Any catalog search by subject requires you to be creative. Even if you find some books on Perón under one subheading, you should check any other subheadings that seem promising. It is much better to come away from the card catalog with too many titles than with too few.

The On-Line Computer Catalog

The computerized catalog is created by putting the information on the 3″ × 5″ catalog cards into electronic form. As a result, the on-line catalog is in many ways organized like the old card catalog. This is especially true for searches by author and title. The principal difference is that instead of flipping through rows of 3″ × 5″ cards, you are typing at a keyboard. Searches by subject are also similar to those in the card catalog, but with the computer you can usually narrow your search to your key word (or words) more easily. The computerized catalog usually has a printer next to it so that you can print out the information that appears on the screen.

One problem with on-line catalogs, however, is that they may contain information on material in *other libraries* as well as your own. An on-line catalog that includes material in other libraries will give you access to many more books, journals, and newspapers, but you will have to go through the process of *borrowing* the materials you need from other libraries. This can be a time-consuming process. Another problem with the on-line catalog is its limited coverage. Usually it contains only the material that the library acquired *after a certain date.* The library may have begun computerizing its holdings in 1975. It may not yet have gotten around to the large task of entering its older material. As a result, your computer search may only turn up the material your library has received on your topic since 1975. If an important book was published earlier, you will have to check the card catalog to find it. One final point: if you are spelling any of your key words wrong, you will get very strange results from your computer terminal.

Searching the On-Line Catalog by Subject

Some on-line catalogs will only allow you to search by author and title. Most, however, will also let you search by subject or, in our case, by key word. If your topic is the forced collectivization of agriculture under Stalin, the computer (with the proper instructions from you) can list on the screen all of the books in its memory whose titles contain the words *collectivization, agriculture,* and *Stalin.* This requires a very close match between all the key words of your topic and the books searched for. If the catalog doesn't contain any books with titles this close to your topic (or if it turns up only one or two), you need to broaden your search. Try exploring a larger area of the computer's memory by asking it to list the books whose titles contain the word *Stalin* whether or not they also contain the words *collectivization* or *agriculture.* This may give you too many titles—several hundred perhaps. At this point, you can slog through the list looking for those titles that sound close to your topic. (*Stalin's Contribution to the Literature on National Minorities* is far from your topic. However, *Stalin and the Peasant Question* is one you should look at.) Knowing how to narrow or broaden a subject search is very important on the computerized catalog. If *Stalin* alone is too broad (too many books on unrelated topics) and all three key words together is too narrow (no books on your specific topic), then the solution, of course, is to pick a term somewhere in between these two. Your other key words (*collectivization, agriculture*) are also too broad. Entering *agriculture*, for example, will get you every book in the library that has anything to do with agriculture, including books such as *Dry Farming: Agriculture in the Great American Desert.*

If each of your key words by itself gives you too many titles unrelated to your topic, then you need to use a heading-subheading combination. This way you ask the computer to break down the large topic into a narrower one, one closer to the topic you are researching. You could try the combinations "Stalin—Agriculture" or "Agriculture—Collectivization." (Some systems will ask for subheadings in the form "Stalin *and* Agricultural" or "Stalin/Agriculture," or some other variation.) Keep playing around with your key words until you get a list that is of appropriate size and contains works that come as close to your topic as you can get.

In the following example, you are looking for books for a paper entitled "Spanish Colonial Rule in America." Entering the key word *America* gives you too many titles; even the heading-subheading "America—Spain" or "Spain—History" still gives you too many. After a few tries, you discover that a *three*-part heading "Spain—Colonies—America" turns out to be about right. It gives you twenty-two titles, each concerning some aspect of your topic. (See Screen A.) Each screen lists about eleven books within this subject category, and Screen A contains numbers 1 through 11 of the twenty-two books found by the computer.

You need to decide which of these books you want to examine further. Several titles look promising, such as numbers 3 and 9. Number 8 is also a good bet. To get more information on this book, enter 8 on the Command line. The result is Screen B, which tells you everything about *Spain in America* that you would find in the card catalog. In addition, it tells you whether the book is checked out or not. Copy down all of the relevant information—author, title, publisher, date, call number—just as you would from the card catalog. Be sure also to copy down the information under the heading "Subjects." These are the three subject headings under which this book is to be found in the on-line catalog. After noting the information for each of the books under "Spain—Colonies—America" that seem likely prospects, begin another subject search using "America—History—To 1810" and another one using "America—Civilization—Spanish Influences." These two searches will

```
Search Request: S=Spain—Colonies—America
Search Results: 22 Entries Found
-------------------------------------------------
     (Spain—Colonies—America/cont.)
 1   Aztecs Under Spanish Rule: A History of t
 2   Bureaucrats of Buenos Aires, 1769-1810
 3   Colonial Latin America
 4   Crisis and Decline: The Viceroyalty of Pe
 5   Government and Society in Colonial Peru:
 6   Kingdom of Quito in the Seventeenth Centu
 7   Maya Society Under Colonial Rule
 8   Spain in America
 9   Spanish Colonial Administration, 1782-181
10   Spanish Struggle for Justice in the Conqu
11   Spanish Theory of Empire in the Sixteenth
-------------------------------------------------
Next Command:
```

Screen A

```
Search Request: S=Spain—Colonies—America
Book: #8 of 22 Entries Found
-------------------------------------------------

TITLE:          Spain in America
AUTHOR:         Gibson, Charles
PUB:            New York, Harper & Row, 1966
SUBJECTS:       Spain—Colonies—America
                America—History—To 1810
                America—Civilization—Spanish
                  Influences
DESCRIPTION:    xiv, 239 p.illus., maps, 22 cm
CALL NUMBER:    Main Library  E18.82 G44
STATUS:         Not Checked Out


-------------------------------------------------
Next Command:
```

Screen B

turn up many of the same books as the first search. However, they will also turn up new ones that may relate to your topic. When you find *one* book that seems useful, always follow the subject leads it furnishes.

Searching On-Line for "Nonbooks"—Journal Articles, Newspapers, Magazines, Microforms, and More

Much of this kind of material is being transferred to computers and, if possible, you should first search for nonbook items in the on-line catalog or in one of the history *databases* that will be described in the sections that follow. If your library does not have databases available, then check the card catalog or the library's separate catalog for nonbook items.

Searching Databases

A database is an electronic list of printed or non-printed materials. Some are like library catalogs and contain lists of books, articles or other publications. Others are very different and contain the articles or documents themselves. Normally, a library will have a section set aside for the computer monitors that display each database. You should become familiar with the contents of the databases in your library.

Most databases can be searched by subject and include instructions. Come to them armed with your key words, but first check any peculiarities of their subject organization. Searching a database by subject may be different than searching a subject in the card or on-line catalogs. If you can't figure out the instructions for using the database, ask the librarian for help.

When you use databases to search for material on your topic, be aware that these electronic lists may go well beyond the holdings of your own library. A database of scholarly journals may give you articles in journals that your library does not own. The easiest way to find out what your own library has in the way of journals is to look at yet another catalog or list. Most libraries have a bound printout that lists all the journals in its collection and the range of years of each journal. If the databases lead you to articles in journals not owned by your library, you can usually borrow them from another library. If your library can receive material from outside electronically, you may be able to receive the specific article you want very quickly—often for a fee. The point to remember is that you should not expect to find all the material listed in databases in your own library, especially if yours is a small one. Whenever you have a choice of databases, be sure to find out from the librarian which ones will be most helpful to you.

Databases for History Research

History databases are of many types. Some list books and are similar to the on-line and card catalogs. Most, however, contain nonbook material, especially articles from journals, magazines, and newspapers. (The most useful history databases are described in Appendix A, section XI of this book.) Some databases are statistical. These contain demographic (population), economic, or political data. They may tell you the population of Paris at various points in the nineteenth century or the number of tons of sugar shipped from Cuba to Boston in 1756. Some databases contain not simply lists of articles but also *annotations* (brief descriptions) of them. Annotations are very helpful in determining which articles are directly related to your topic. Finally, some databases are "whole text" databases. These contain not only lists of articles but *the articles themselves*. This latter kind of database is just coming into use. Most "whole text" databases are *CD-ROM* discs. These can include not only whole articles but the contents of encyclopedias, collections of maps, photographs, paintings (and other art objects), or copies of historical documents. The latest addition to library research are CD-ROM discs that contain films, computer animations, musical scores, and whole collections of books that you can read sitting at the terminal. You will probably not find this newest technology (known as Multimedia or Hypermedia) in your library yet. If you do, ask the librarian how you can use it to do historical research.

Reference Books—Indexes to Articles and Documents

The final path into the library's material on your topic is its collection of reference books. The reference section of your library (usually located near the card catalog, on-line catalog, and databases) is composed of encyclopedias, dictionaries, atlases, directories, indexes, official documents, and much more. The uses of these kinds of reference works for historical research are explained in Appendix A, sections I through VI. Two of the most valuable reference books are *periodical indexes* and *newspaper indexes*. Periodical indexes list articles in scholarly journals and popular magazines by subject. Newspaper indexes each cover one newspaper and list each article that appeared by subject and date. *Indexes of government documents* are another valuable research tool. These list published reports by city, county, state, national, and international bodies. They are usually organized by the name of the government agency, by subject matter, and by date.

Each index has its own way of organizing its contents. You will need to read the rules for using the index that appear at the beginning of the volume. The librarian should be helpful in determining which of these indexes will lead you to information on your topic.

Reference Books—Microprint Sources

Some reference books list and describe materials that have been photographed and miniaturized in forms such as microfilm and microfiche. Many libraries have collections of this kind of material containing old books, magazines, newspapers, or documents. These materials often have their own catalog or have special designations when they are included in the card or on-line catalogs. Your library may also have collections of photographs, movies, records, audio and videotapes, and oral history transcripts or recordings. (For a listing of guides to microprint sources of information, see Appendix A, section IX.)

Reference Books—Subject Bibliographies

The most important part of the reference collection are its *subject bibliographies*. These comprise a path into the materials of the library just as important as the card and on-line catalogs. In fact, a large part of the book you are reading (see Appendix A, section VII) is dedicated to helping you find the subject bibliographies that will be most helpful in finding books (and other materials) on your topic.

Subject bibliographies list books, articles, and other materials according to subject. Their contents are confined to the subject indicated in their title. To aid you in your research, this book lists several hundred subject bibliographies separating them by historical period, area, or topic. You should keep in mind, of course, that, like databases, not all of the material listed in these bibliographies will be in your school library. Despite this fact, a subject bibliography that lists books and other material related to your topic is often the best place to begin research. The task is made easier for you because you can start your research in Appendix A of this book. Much of what you need to research your topic may be discovered in this way. For example, if your topic is the use of chemical weapons in the Vietnam War, the subject bibliography *The Wars in Vietnam, Cambodia, and Laos, 1945–1982: A Bibliographic Guide* (listed in Appendix A, section VII, L. 2. "Southeast Asian History") may lead you to many sources of information on your topic.

One advantage to using subject bibliographies is that you have already narrowed your search by choosing one that covers your topic. Another advantage is that after you go to the section or sections of the reference book that seem closest to your topic, you can *browse* through the rest of the volume to see what other headings and subheadings sound promising. This is more difficult to do with the on-line and card catalogs. Also, many subject bibliographies are annotated. They list the titles of books or articles and also briefly describe their contents. This is very helpful. Finally, a subject bibliography, unlike the on-line catalog, will have older books as well as recent ones. If it has been recently published or updated, it will list very new works as well. Of course, a bibliography compiled in 1965 will not contain material published later. Keep this in mind.

There is no one best way to conduct library research. Each of the three paths described here is useful and has its own strengths and weaknesses. Your research goal should not be to find *enough* information on your topic but the *best* information on your topic. An element of the grade you receive for your history paper will be based upon the quality of your sources.

Locating Materials and Using Call Numbers

After completing your search of the card and computer catalogs and of the subject bibliographies, you will have a list of materials that you want to look at. If some of these are located outside your library, you will have to borrow them. A librarian will have to assist you in this task. If the materials are in your own library, the call number will lead you to them. The call numbers in use in almost all libraries are of one of two types: the Dewey Decimal System or the Library of Congress System. The Dewey call numbers begin with a *number;* the Library of Congress call numbers begin with a *letter.* These are both complex systems of organizing books by subject. However, if you go to the trouble of mastering their principles, you will have an excellent road map to your library's shelves. (An explanation of the Dewey Decimal and the Library of Congress classification systems can be found in Appendix B.)

If the stacks are open to students, pay attention to the signs on the walls and at the ends of rows of shelves that tell you where a particular group of call numbers is to be found. If you get to the place in the shelves where you think the book should be and it is not there, you are facing one of several problems: (1) the book has been taken out by another reader; (2) it has been shelved incorrectly; (3) you have copied down the call number incorrectly; or (4) it has been lost or stolen. Often an on-line catalog will tell you if a book has been taken out by someone else. This is one of the advantages of a computer search. In any event, the circulation desk librarian can tell you if another reader has checked it out. If it has not been checked out, go back to the catalog and check the call number. An error of even one number in a call number can make your search all but impossible. Always be sure to copy call numbers letter by letter and number by number just as they appear in the catalog.

Browsing the Library Shelves

Most of the call numbers on the list you have created will be in groups. They will begin with similar letters and numbers. All of the books with similar call numbers will be near one another on the library's shelves. As a result, when you get to the place in the stacks where one book is located it will be surrounded by other books with very similar call numbers. Since the system of filing books by call number is related to their subject, nearby books may also be on your list. Just as important, nearby books that are not on your list may be just as close to your topic as those that are. Read the titles of the books near to the one you are seeking. If the titles seem promising, they should be added to your list.

Determining Whether a Book Will Be Useful

Once you have a book in your hand, you can now find out if it contains the kind of information on your topic that you are looking for. Up to this point you have been relying on book titles. Now you can go through the book's table of contents and the index at the end. These are much better guides to the book's contents. After all, titles can be misleading. *The Election of Woodrow Wilson* may turn out to be about the inner workings of the Democratic Party. If you are preparing a paper on Wilson, this book may not be of much use to you, despite its title. Even when a book deals specifically with your topic, its handling of the subject may make it less than satisfactory. For example, a book that is written for less advanced students, even though it is on your topic, will not make a good source. Its coverage will be too general, and it will also likely gloss over or omit important facts or interpretations that your research should include. You should avoid textbooks or works that seem to be written more for entertainment than information. If the author does not include footnotes and a bibliography, the book may not be a proper source for a research paper. A glance at the introduction should help you determine the kind of reader for whom the book was written.

Another problem you may encounter is the author's viewpoint or bias. For example, a history of World War I by a French author is likely to have a different viewpoint from one written by a German author, especially if the books were written close to the time of the war. It is very important for you to understand the point of view from which a book was written. Many historical events and their interpretation are the centers of profound controversy. It is almost impossible for a historian to investigate one of these controversial areas without the involvement of certain biases. A particular attitude toward the topic is not necessarily bad, however. Historical problems are immensely complex, and without a sense of which things are important, the historian will not be able to choose from among those facts that can give some clear meaning to the larger questions involved. In any event, it is important for you to become familiar with the biases of the authors you read so that you will not unknowingly accept their viewpoints. If you agree with an author's bias, it is natural that you will favor his or her work in your research. But unless you understand the biases of the authors you read, and your own as well, you will not know why you agree with some authors more than others. Furthermore, you won't be able to make a logical presentation in your research paper of the varying points of view.

The first place to check for determining the usefulness and emphasis of a book is its table of contents. Although some chapter titles are vague, most will give you a clearer picture of the contents than the work's title. If your topic is the Caribbean policy of Theodore Roosevelt, and you have come upon a book entitled *The Era of Theodore Roosevelt,* you will be pleased to find a chapter called "Hemisphere Diplomacy." Though the entire work may be of value to you, it is this chapter that will contain the most material on your specific topic. On the other hand, if the chapter headings are all concerned with Roosevelt's domestic policies or the cultural, scientific, and intellectual trends of the early 1900s, there may be little in the book on foreign policy.

If the chapter headings are not clear enough for you to determine the book's usefulness, read the index. Not every book has an index, but when one does, it is an invaluable tool. The index lists in alphabetical order the pages on which different persons or subjects are discussed. The index in a book on the Progressive Party in Wisconsin will list each of the pages on which Robert M. LaFollette is mentioned. It may even break this down and tell you which pages discuss LaFollette's early career, which discuss his campaigns for the presidency, and so on. When the scope of a book is very broad, the index is the best guide to finding that portion of it that is closest to your topic. Remember, however, that unless you read more of the book than just those pages that deal with your topic, you will not know the author's biases or conclusions, and these may be of great importance. Although you may want to select only small portions of a book to use in your research, if any of your own conclusions are drawn from a particular work, you will need to know its overall contents.

If the book has no index, or if you wish to get the flavor of the work as a whole before selecting it as a source for your paper, the introduction and bibliography may be of help. Authors often explain some of their purposes and conclusions in the introduction, and a look at the bibliography (if one is included) will give clues as to what sources the author felt were important and how extensive his or her own research was.

Perhaps the best way to gain an overall impression of a work is to skim its contents by reading the introductory paragraph of each chapter and perhaps the introductory sentence to each paragraph in those parts of the book that seem most important. If you have mastered a method of rapid reading, that skill will be very useful here. Once you have chosen a book for your research, of course, there is no substitute for careful reading.

Reading Books

Reading books may sound easy, but, unless you have had experience in reading serious historical studies, you may have problems. First of all, some of the vocabulary may be new to you. A book on the French Revolution will contain such words as *Jacobin, Thermidor,* and *Girondin.* A study of the atom bomb will talk about implosion and fission and such places as Tinian and Eniwetok. It is best to have a good dictionary handy. Another problem will be the academic or scholarly style of writing often found in specialized works. You will come across sentences like this:

> Despite the innumerable, and often contradictory, intellectual themes reflected in the ideological position taken by the right wing of the movement, it nevertheless managed, despite the defection of a small fascist element, to maintain the loyalty of the land-owning peasantry of the Central Highlands as well as the professional and shopowners associations of the capital, not to mention that of several union organizations that still maintained a craft orientation.

By the time you finish such a sentence, you may have forgotten how it began. To make matters worse, such tongue twisters are often filled with words like: *balkanization, corporativism, Hegelianism, Mandate of Heaven, negritude, neomercantilism, Pan-Slavism, Pax Romana, popular front, primogeniture, Reconquista, shogunate, Trotskyism, utilitariansim, White Terror,* or *Zoroastrianism.* Unfortunately there is no shortcut to understanding such terminology. As you become familiar with your topic, you will learn the meanings of the terms used by scholars. The only way to get through the complex prose is to have a good command of English grammar and a familiarity with the subject being discussed.

Therefore, among the books you have chosen for your research, you should read first the most general and then the more specialized ones. As you become familiar with the style and terminology used in a work, your main task will be to understand the points the author is trying to establish. All good works of history do more than just lay out a series of historical events and then combine them to form an understandable story of what occurred. Good historians want to prove a point, to show that a series of historical events mean one thing rather than another. A history of the rise of Adolf Hitler won't merely tell you that the National Socialist Party, which he led, increased the number of its representatives in the German Reichstag (parliament) from 12 to 107 in the election of 1930. It will attempt to describe the conditions that led to such an outcome and to explain the impact of the election on later events. Perhaps the author will discuss unemployment, German nationalism, the cartelization of German industry, the Treaty of Versailles, the growth of the German Communist Party, anti-Semitism, the structure of the German family, the philosophy of Nietzsche, or the insecurity of the lower middle class. The author will probably deal with some of these more extensively than others, and will attempt to show how the emphasized factors offer a better explanation of the subject than any others. Although almost all historians will agree on the number of National Socialist members of the 1930 Reichstag, each will construct the causes and effects of that fact in different ways—sometimes in *very* different ways. If you wish to understand a particular author's interpretation of an event, you must know how the author arrived at that interpretation and what significance he or she believes it to have. Only a careful reading of the entire work and close attention to the book's main arguments can give you such knowledge. Remember, history books are a selection of certain facts and interpretations constructed to explain a particular writer's understanding of a historical subject. If your own research relies heavily on a particular book, you will need to know its theme and bias.

Taking Notes

The first rule in note taking is to know in advance what you are looking for. In order to avoid either taking note after note that you will never need or failing to note things that you will, you should have a clear understanding of your topic and the kind of evidence you are seeking. This is especially difficult at the outset of your research when your understanding of your topic is still somewhat vague. It is thus important to define the scope and content of your topic as quickly as possible or your research and note taking will wander, and valuable time will be lost.

As you go through a book, you will find portions that you will want to refer to in your own research paper. You will want to note the author's general idea or perhaps even record the actual words used. If you wish to quote, be careful to copy exactly the words in the book. Be sure that the meaning of the words you quote is clear and that you have not altered the author's point by quoting it out of context. If you wish to use a quotation, say, to show that Robert E. Lee was a good military strategist, a quotation such as "Lee was more admired by the average soldier than any other commanding officer" doesn't make that point because it refers to his popularity, not his generalship. Moreover, if the following sentence in the book is "However, his strategic decisions were not usually equal to those of Union army commanders," then you have actually altered the author's point by taking it out of its original context. Make sure you understand the author's meaning before you use a quotation. Also, be sure not to overquote. Do not quote more material than is necessary to convey the desired point clearly and accurately. Finally, never quote something simply because you find it difficult to express in your own words. You will have to compose the idea in your own words when you write your paper, and it is best to think about the meaning of your research material now.

The most important points made by an author usually cannot be summed up in easily quotable form. When you want to record general arguments and conclusions, it is best to write your own paraphrase or summary of particular points. If the author has spent several pages relating the decline in trade between Spain and Mexico to the Wars of Mexican Independence, you may want to summarize the findings by noting that the author feels that the diminishing economic tie between colony and mother country was one of the major factors leading to Mexican independence. If you wish to note the evidence itself, you may want to paraphrase the author's description of the decline in trade with several sentences of your own that include the main factors of this decline.

Whether you are quoting an author's exact words or summarizing a point, the rules of note taking are the same. As you read, it is best to have a pile of index cards beside you (4" × 6" or 5" × 8", not 3" × 5"). When you come to something you want to note, write the author's name, the book title, and the page number or numbers at the top of the card.[2] The exact page numbers are essential because you will have to use

---

[2]If you are taking notes on a journal or newspaper article, you will need to record such information as date, volume number, page, and column number.

them when you write your footnotes. If your quote or paraphrase covers more than one page from your source, be sure to make that fact clear on your note card. Also, it is essential to place each paraphrase or quotation on a separate card so that you can arrange them by date or topic when you prepare your paper. Placing a brief topic heading in the corner of each card will make such arrangement easier. (See examples of note cards on page 74.)

If you are quoting, be sure to use quotation marks and to copy the quotation word for word. If you are quoting something that the author has quoted, you must be sure to point this out when you use the material and to identify the original source. Be sure to include in your note an introduction to the quoted material in your own words, stating who said it (if other than the author) and in what context. This will ensure that you use it properly in your paper. If a quotation is very long and if there are parts that relate to matters other than the one you are referring to, then you may omit portions of the original quote by inserting ellipses—three periods (. . .)—in the quoted material.[3] For example, if the quotation reads "Feudalism, despite later idealizations of it, was maintained by an oppressive social order," you may want to leave out "despite later idealizations of it," and quote the sentence as "Feudalism . . . was maintained by an oppressive social order." However, never omit anything if doing so would change the meaning of the material. If the sentence had read "Feudalism in its later stages in Moravia was maintained by an oppressive social order," the entire sentence would have to be quoted, or its meaning would be seriously altered.

To give a clearer sense of what note taking involves, there are two sample note cards on p. 74. The first contains a quotation from a book and the second a paraphrasing of several paragraphs from an article.

Avoiding Plagiarism

The only thing worse than misquoting from your sources is plagiarizing from them. Plagiarism is easy to fall into. Because of your inexperience with your subject, it will be tempting to use the more sophisticated language of the historians you are reading. In most cases, their expertise will enable them to make their point clearly, and it is easy to get into the habit of using their words instead of your own. Don't fall into this trap. First of all, your instructor is also a historian and can tell the difference between the language of someone who has spent years researching a

---

[3]If the portion omitted is the end of a sentence, this is indicated by inserting four periods—three to indicate omission and the fourth to indicate the end of the original sentence. In this case, the closing quotation mark appears after the fourth period.

Sample Note Cards

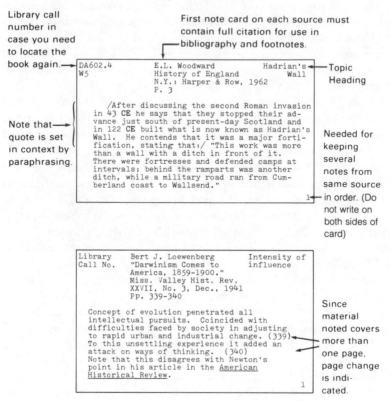

Library call
number in
case you need
to locate the
book again.➞

First note card on each source must
contain full citation for use in
┌─bibliography and footnotes.

```
DA602.4      E.L. Woodward          Hadrian's◄─Topic
W5           History of England         Wall
             N.Y.: Harper & Row, 1962              Heading
             P. 3
```

Note that➞
quote is set
in context by
paraphrasing.

```
/After discussing the second Roman invasion
in 43 CE he says that they stopped their ad-
vance just south of present-day Scotland and
in 122 CE built what is now known as Hadrian's
Wall.  He contends that it was a major forti-
fication, stating that:/ "This work was more
than a wall with a ditch in front of it.
There were fortresses and defended camps at
intervals; behind the ramparts was another
ditch, while a military road ran from Cum-
berland coast to Wallsend."
                                              1◄─
```

Needed for
keeping
several
notes from
same source
in order. (Do
not write on
both sides of
card)

```
Library      Bert J. Loewenberg       Intensity of
Call No.     "Darwinism Comes to      influence
             America, 1859-1900."
             Miss. Valley Hist. Rev.
             XXVII, No. 3, Dec., 1941
             Pp. 339-340

Concept of evolution penetrated all
intellectual pursuits.  Coincided with
difficulties faced by society in adjusting
to rapid urban and industrial change. (339)◄
To this unsettling experience it added an   ◄
attack on ways of thinking. (340)
Note that this disagrees with Newton's
point in his article in the American
Historical Review.
                                           1
```

Since
material
noted covers
more than
one page,
page change
is indi-
cated.

topic and that of the average history student. Second, and more important, is the fact that thinking is learning. If you substitute the simple task
of copying for the more difficult but rewarding one of thinking about
something and then putting it into your own words, then you are doing
yourself a disservice.

To help you avoid plagiarism, here is a passage from J. Joseph
Hutchmaker and Warren I. Sussman, eds., *Wilson's Diplomacy: An International Symposium* (Cambridge, Mass.: Schenckman, 1973), p. 13,
followed by two paraphrasings. Paraphrase *a* constitutes plagiarism, but
b does not. The subject is the diplomacy of Woodrow Wilson. Here is
the original text:

> Wilson took personal responsibility for the conduct of the
> important diplomacy of the United States chiefly because

he believed that it was wise, right, and necessary for him to do so. Believing as he did that the people had temporarily vested their sovereignty in foreign affairs in him, he could not delegate responsibility in this field to any individual. His scholarly training and self-disciplined habits of work made him so much more efficient than his advisers that he must have thought that the most economical way of doing important diplomatic business was for him to do it himself. Experience in dealing with subordinates who sometimes tried to defeat his purposes also led him to conclude that it was the safest method, for he, and not his subordinates, bore the responsibility to the American people and to history for the consequences of his policies.

Paraphrase a

Wilson took personal responsibility for conducting diplomacy because he believed it was right for him to do so. Believing that the people had vested their sovereignty in foreign affairs in him, he couldn't delegate this responsibility. His scholarly training and self-discipline made him more efficient than his advisers. He thought that the most economical way of doing important business was to do it himself. Experience in dealing with subordinates who sometimes tried to defeat his purposes led him to conclude that it was the safest method because he bore responsibility to the American people for the consequences.

Paraphrase b

Wilson felt personally responsible for major diplomacy because he believed that the voters had entrusted him with such matters. He was more capable than his advisers in this area. He, and not his advisers, was responsible to the people.

Paraphrase *a* is too close to the original. Rather than recording the main points of the passage, it repeats many phrases word for word. Not only is it time consuming to take such lengthy notes, but the identical and almost identical phrases, if used as your own, would constitute plagiarism. The second paraphrase records only the principal point of the passage—that Wilson decided major foreign policy issues on his own because he felt personally responsible to the people in such matters. It does not copy the phraseology of the original. In this way, you save time, avoid plagiarism, and still are able to use the central idea of the passage. Paraphrasing that reduces your readings to their essential points and utilizes your own words is not easy at first. But mastering this technique will prevent plagiarism and produce a finished paper that is truly yours.

Outlining and Organizing

While you are conducting your research and gathering your notes, you may be tentatively organizing and even writing parts of your paper. But when your research is finished, you must put your outline in its final form and organize your numerous note cards accordingly.

If your topic is African Americans and the Depression, you may decide to deal with the topic chronologically and separate your paper into sections dealing with the period before 1929, the Hoover years, the early New Deal, and the late New Deal. Or perhaps you want to cover the subject topically, setting up separate sections on African-American reactions to economic discrimination, the National Association for the Advancement of Colored People, the U.S. Communist Party, organized labor, and New Deal legislation. Or perhaps you will want to consider the ideas of important African-American leaders and writers of the day, setting up sections dealing with E. Franklin Frazier, Richard Wright, Ralph Bunche, W. E. B. Du Bois, A. Philip Randolph, Langston Hughes, Zora Neal Hurston, and Claude McKay.

A chronological approach begins with events that predate those that are the main focus of the paper. It then moves, step by step, through stages that group together spans of time. These spans may be in years, decades, or—for a very broad topic—centuries. Each time span is later than the one preceding it, and they generally do not overlap.

Time spans do not have to be the same length. It is best to use larger time units when discussing events that occurred long before the main events covered in the paper and to use smaller units when covering the period closest to the main events. A different rule applies to the length of each *section* of the paper: those portions dealing with periods removed from central events should be briefer than those portions close in time to such events.

A common problem with chronological organization is determining how far back in time to begin. Do you start ten or a hundred years before the time of the main events of the paper? A similar problem is determining where to stop. Do you stop with the main events themselves, or do you add sections covering later periods as well? There is no hard and fast rule, but it is wise not to cover too much ground. That is, don't start too long before or end too long after the principal events of your topic. A paper covering several hundred years is very unwieldy, and is best not handled by the chronological form of organization.

A topical form of organization is usually best for more general themes—those that deal with ideas, social systems, or other complex phenomena that involve a mixture of political, social, economic, cultural, and intellectual backgrounds. In this form of organization, the task is not so much to build a historical sequence leading up to a particular event, but to weave a fabric composed of the many separate lines of historical development that form the background to the main topic. In many cases, the same topic can be organized by either method. If you have trouble choosing, or if you wish to explore other forms, your instructor should be able to help you.

To give you an idea of how a particular topic might be organized by each of the two methods, here are sample tables of contents of two papers called "The United States and the War in Vietnam."

Chronologically:

Introduction
I. The United States and the French War in Vietnam, 1946–1954
II. The Geneva Conference of 1954
III. The Eisenhower Administration and the South Vietnamese Government of Ngo Dinh Diem, 1954–1960
IV. Military Involvement Under President Kennedy, 1961–1963
V. Escalation Under President Johnson, 1964–1968
VI. Negotiation and Troop Withdrawals Under President Nixon, 1969–1973
VII. Conclusion—The United States and Vietnam Today

Topically:

Introduction
I. United States Economic and Political Interests in Vietnam
II. The History of Communism in Vietnam
III. United States Foreign Policy and Vietnam
IV. Congress and the War
V. The Antiwar Movement in the United States
VI. The Politics of the Republic of South Vietnam
VII. The Vietnam War and International Relations
VIII. Conclusion

However you choose to organize your paper, you must organize your notes in the same manner. One of the best ways to do this is to read each of your note cards and mark it according to that part of the paper to which it applies. You may also want to describe briefly the contents of each card at the top. Then, when you prepare the final organization of your paper, you can arrange all your notes within each section according to the subjects to which they refer. (See Chapter 5, the section on "Organization.")

Budgeting Research Time

If you are writing, say, a fifteen- to thirty-page paper, expect to read about a dozen sources. This is not a firm figure, however, and your teacher and the subject you choose are the best guides to the proper amount of research. If you read too few sources, your work will be shallow and perhaps unsatisfactory. If you read too many, you will not complete your work in the allotted time. It is best to make a tentative bibliography early in your research and discuss its adequacy in terms of topicality, authoritativeness, and length with your instructor. In addition, discuss with your teacher the preliminary outline for your paper.

If you have never written a long research paper before, you may be unsure as to how much time to allow for each aspect of your research and writing. Only experience will tell you the best budget of time for your particular work habits, but here are some general rules.

For a paper of fifteen to thirty pages due at the end of a fifteen-week semester, you should allow approximately 10 percent of your time (one to two weeks) for choosing a topic, preparing a tentative bibliography, and familiarizing yourself with the general contours of your topic; about 60 percent (seven to eight weeks) for reading the available research materials and taking notes from them; about 10 percent (another week) for thinking and talking about what you have read and organizing your notes; and about 20 percent (two to four weeks) for writing and typing the preliminary and final drafts.

If your term is much shorter than fifteen weeks, or if your assignment must be finished before the end of the semester, you will need to shorten your budget accordingly. (For a discussion of the preparation of papers of five to fifteen pages, see Chapter 3.) Remember that by the end of the term, exams will dominate your attention, and a paper due the final week of classes is best finished at least a week before that time so as not to conflict with studying for finals.

Historical Materials outside the Library

If you are fortunate, your topic will be one on which special historical materials are available at a nearby special collections library, a museum, a historical society, the archives of an institution or corporation, or film and audiotape libraries of television and radio studios.

Older members of your community or your own family also can be sources of historical information. People who have been leaders in local and national affairs have personal knowledge of important historical events. Perhaps you could prepare a series of questions concerning past events in which they were participants. You can write to these individuals, or perhaps speak with them. They may also have personal papers they would permit you to see. This kind of historical research is exciting and satisfying, and it may enable you to use primary historical material that no other historian has uncovered.

Elderly people are very good sources of historical material. They can tell of their years in another country or describe the America in which they grew up. They may not have been important historical figures, but they reflect the experiences of countless others and are thus the stuff of which history is made. Their recollections of how they felt and of what they and others did and said when, for example, the *Titanic* sank, when women won the right to vote, when Lindbergh flew across the Atlantic, or when Babe Ruth hit a record-breaking home run are priceless pieces of the historical puzzle. (See also Appendix B, the section on "Historical Sources in Your Backyard.")

How to Research Your Family History

One of the most pleasurable kinds of historical research is the composition of your own family's history. Moreover, to research it is to re-create a portion of the historical experience of our nation. Because most of our ancestors came from other nations, a family history also will connect us with the historical experience of other lands. By studying the history of your family, you become aware of your own place within these broader historical experiences. Perhaps most important, knowledge of your family's history and its meaning can give you a strong sense of your cultural roots that will strengthen you throughout your lifetime.

The best sources—and in many cases the only sources—of information on the history of your family are the recollections, understandings, and long-term possessions of your relatives. Researching a family history involves investigating these sources as thoroughly and creatively as possible. Rather than mastering the theme or weighing the evidence of a group of historical monographs or primary documents, research in this instance takes three forms: (1) familiarizing yourself with the general history of the nations and regions, and of the specific times and places, in which your ancestors lived; (2) studying all available family records, such as diaries, photographs, heirlooms; and finally, and most important, (3) interviewing all available family members.

The interview is the core of a family history because, in most instances, it is the only way of uncovering the nature of your family's life. Without the recollections of your relations, you would not be able to discover more than a handful of names, dates, and places—only the barest outline of your family's history.

In preparing for this crucial aspect of family research, you must familiarize yourself with the basic history of your family so that you can place in proper context the information you obtain from the people you interview. You will need to prepare your questions beforehand, focusing on important aspects of family life and of the larger social and political life surrounding the family. Be sure that your questions establish the basics: the names, relationships, and principal home and workplace activities of each member of the family in each generation, going as far down the trunk and out on the limbs of the family tree as possible given the scope of your project and the memories of your relatives. Keep away from trivia (your great-uncle's favorite dessert), and look for information that will enable you to make comparisons between generations of your family and between it and other families. Investigate such topics as the type of dwelling and neighborhood, parent-child and husband-wife relationships, authority and status patterns, income and social mobility. When you come across major family events—immigration, military service, job and residence changes, involvement in political movements—probe the reasons for them, as they will illuminate the ties between your family and the nation's history.

In actually conducting the interview, use your prepared questions, taking care to make them as broad as possible; for example, "What was the neighborhood like when you lived there?" not "What was your address in 1936?" When you get an answer that seems to lead in the direction of important material, ignore your prepared questions temporarily and probe further. However, never interrupt an answer, even when the response seems unimportant. Your informants are the experts on their lives, and their self-perceptions—even if illogical or factually incorrect—are essential ingredients of family history. Finally, because the intricate web of your relatives' feelings is as important as the milestones of their lives, it is best to tape-record the interview if possible rather than rely on written notes. Record it all and then collect from your tapes the information which, on the one hand, best reflects your informants' testimony about their lives and, on the other, enables you to say something of importance about those lives and the times in which they were lived.

chapter 5

How to Write
a Research Paper

The Theme

It is impossible to write a complete history of your topic, and you should not try. A good research paper will give the basic facts and interpretations concerning a subject, but it should not become a record of everything you have read.[1] Your aim in writing a history research paper is to use your knowledge of the topic to develop a particular *theme*—a central point, assertion, or argument for the facts and interpretations of your paper. The goal of your writing should be to introduce the theme clearly, support it effectively, and then draw meaningful conclusions about it.

Instead of merely describing the life of someone, the course of a war, or the outcome of an election, your paper should take a stand and make

---

[1]This chapter contains generally accepted guides to writing style. Check to see if your instructor has any specific preferences that may vary from these.

assertions. For example, a paper on the siege of the Alamo should do more than tell the story of the battle. It should make some central point about the siege and argue its importance. Your instructor will not be satisfied with a paper that describes the nature of the fortifications, relates how many died, and concludes that the defenders were very brave. You must find some theme that explains the causes of the battle or that relates the event to larger issues. Perhaps you will want to discuss the morale of both forces and relate the course and outcome of the battle to the fighting ability of the Mexican army or to the cause of Texas independence. If your subject is the early career of Jiang Jieshi (Chiang Kai-shek), instead of merely relating the major events of his life, choose a theme such as the effect of the Bolshevik Revolution on his thinking or how his ideas on land reform influenced his relationship with the Chinese Communist Party. With your thematic focus, your facts and arguments become relevant, and your paper develops them logically and clearly.

Organization

You are now prepared to *outline* your paper. Break down your subject into those elements that best illustrate your theme. From your reading, you should be familiar with those aspects of it that were given prominence, or that you yourself have concluded are important. The outline of your paper should include sections that deal with these important areas in a way that relates them to your theme. For example, if your subject is the conflict between Israel and its Arab neighbors, your research may have determined that two basic elements of the subject are Zionism and Arab nationalism, and that two important events were the Balfour Declaration of 1917 and the United Nations Partition Plan of 1947. If most or all of your sources mention these as important, then you must find a place for them in your outline so that you will not fail to cover them in your paper.

When a point is not stressed by your sources but you have concluded that it is of significance to your theme, it should, of course, be included. For example, if your theme is Nasser's commitment to Arab nationalism and, after researching the Arab-Israeli dispute, you conclude that Nasser's reaction to his experiences in the war of 1948 was an important factor in his later conduct, then, even if your sources treated this matter very lightly, you will want it to appear in your outline.

When constructing an outline, be sure that you have enough facts to support each separate item. You cannot deal effectively with the issue of Nasser's experience in 1948 unless your notes contain evidence to support your point of view. Although you are free to draw your own conclusions from what you have read, your paper should not emphasize unsupported views you may have. If you feel very strongly about a particular point but don't find it supported by your research, then you must try to find some corroboration for your views. Even without support from other sources, however, you can still state your own opinions in your paper, but they should be clearly labeled as such.

In addition to pursuing your theme and covering the important points made in your reading, your outline should include an introduction and conclusion. The introduction should state the central theme and explain why you think the topic is important or interesting. The conclusion should sum up the major points, explain how they sustain your central theme, and discuss the importance of your theme for other subjects.

When constructing an outline, be sure that the sections are in a logical order. If you are treating your subject chronologically, each part of the outline must be in date order. If you are dividing your subject topically, each topic must raise a separate issue. Always keep in mind that the purpose of your outline is to develop your theme. If your subject is the role of the peasantry in the Mexican Revolution, and your theme is that the peasants' military role was crucial to the outcome of the Revolution, then the political philosophy of the liberal landowner Francisco Madero, regardless of its importance, should not be a part of your outline. Each part of the outline must pass two tests: does it relate to the theme, and does it deal with a different aspect of the theme from the other parts of the outline? (For sample outlines, see page 77.)

Writing the Text

Once you have prepared your outline and separated your notes according to the parts of the outline to which they correspond, you will need to judge how long each section of the paper should be. The length and number of sections will vary according to the subject matter and the type of assignment, but here is a general guide: if your paper is to be about twenty-five pages long, it is best not to have more than six or seven sections. You will need at least three or four pages to treat adequately each of the points you want to cover. As you write the rough draft of each section, keep in mind the information you wish to include and the principal points you wish to develop. Form that section around the corresponding notes, making sure that you explain the relationships among the facts you present.

Your paper as a whole should contain an introduction, a central development (the body), and a conclusion. Likewise, each section should set out its particular point, move through the development of that point, and close with material that relates that point to those that follow. If your topic is German aid to the forces of General Francisco Franco in the Spanish Civil War, then the section that deals with the reasons behind the German support might begin by briefly describing the circumstances surrounding Franco's appeal to Hitler in 1936. The main body of the section would explain in some detail Hitler's reasons for giving aid (for example, strategic and economic considerations, ideological and diplomatic factors) and would conclude by relating these reasons to the subject of later sections, such as the actual aid given and its effect on the course of the war. Your principal concerns as you construct each section of your paper should be: does this section follow logically from the one preceding it; does it adequately support and develop the central theme; and does it establish the necessary background for the section that follows?

As each section mirrors the overall structure of the paper by containing an introduction, development, and conclusion, so each paragraph of which the section is composed contains a similar structure. A well-constructed paragraph begins with a sentence that introduces the information to be developed and concludes with a sentence that summarizes that information. If each paragraph is developed in this way, and if sentences explaining the relationship between paragraphs are included where necessary, then the paper as a whole becomes a tightly knit series of related statements rather than a random group of facts that do not seem to move in any clear direction. The key to tight construction is for each sentence to have two components: it must be related to the one preceding it, and it must continue the development of the theme to which it is related.

Here are two groups of sentences. The first is tightly constructed; the second is not.

> In 1919, most Germans felt that the terms of the Versailles Treaty were harsh. In particular, they believed that the reparations and war-guilt clauses of the Treaty were unjust. When Hitler rose to power fourteen years later, he appealed to this sense of injustice in order to gain support for his program of denouncing the Treaty.

In 1919, most Germans felt that the terms of the Versailles Treaty were harsh. The French hoped to weaken German war-making capacity by forcing her to pay heavy war reparations. Hitler appealed to the German people to support his program to denounce the Treaty.

Although each sentence in the second version is true, the paragraph does not hang together because the sentences are not clearly related. The first sentence refers to German feelings about the treaty, and then the second jumps to a discussion of French attitudes and drops the reference to the Versailles Treaty, which is the common theme that ties together the sentences of the first version. The third sentence further confuses the situation by jumping back to Germany and forward in time without any proper transition. On the other hand, the first version is tightly constructed because the second sentence, rather than breaking the line of development by bringing in a new element, expands and accentuates the point made in the first. The third sentence explains the forward jump in time and relates the events of the later period (Hitler's denunciation of the Treaty) to the German people's sense of injustice established in the first two sentences.

The best way to ensure that there are no logical gaps between your sentences is to construct each paragraph from the viewpoint of the average person who might read your paper. Very often, a disconnected set of sentences may seem clear to you because as you write them you unconsciously fill in the gaps with your own knowledge. Your reader most likely does not have this knowledge and has to depend entirely on the words you write. If these are not enough to make your point clearly, you must be more explicit.[2]

Before you write your final draft, it is often helpful to put your paper aside for a day or two and then reread it. By doing so, you can often gain a fresh perspective and can detect weaknesses that you hadn't noticed before.

Example of a Research Paper

The following is an example of a very well written research paper. It appears here without a title page, footnotes, or bibliography in order to focus your full attention on matters of organization and writing style.

---

[2]The other basic component of clarity is a well-constructed sentence. No matter how well sentences are linked to one another, if the sentences themselves have faulty grammatical construction, the result will be unsatisfactory. If your sentence writing ability is weak, you should study one of the grammar and style manuals listed in Appendix B.

Rules and examples concerning footnotes and bibliography—both essentials of a good research paper—are discussed on subsequent pages. To give you an idea of what sort of statements need to be footnoted, these places have been marked with a footnote number.

To enable you to see the structure of this paper more clearly, the specific function of each group of sentences is indicated in the margin. Note that most sentences fall into one of three categories: (1) *developing the basic theme* set forth in the introduction, (2) giving *evidence* for or an *interpretation* of a particular development of the theme, or (3) serving as a *transition* between two theme developments. The paper concludes with a summary of the theme's development and with the writer's own conclusions. Note that the subheadings serve both as statements of theme development and as transitions.

The Impact of the Scientific Revolution on Moral Philosophy

Introduction

Statement of Theme

This paper shows how changes in knowledge lead to changes in social thought. It investigates the Scientific Revolution in Europe in the seventeenth and eighteenth centuries and the impact of that revolution on religious and moral thinking. The paper will try to show that the Scientific Revolution stimulated great changes in people's thinking about humanity, nature, and religion. However, scientific thought did not replace the older moral and religious teaching. Instead, it combined with them to form new ideas.

I. The Impact of the Scientific Revolution

Thematic Dev.

The scientific discoveries of the seventeenth and eighteenth centuries in Europe were many, and they were fundamental to later scientific developments and to

changes in social thought. These discoveries included the

Evidence

circulation of the blood by William Harvey, the properties

of gases by Robert Boyle, the existence of microscopic

organisms by Anton van Leeuwenhoek, and the nature of

combustion by Antoine Lavoisier.[1] While the origins of

these discoveries can be found in the work of Greek

Thematic Development

thinkers, Arab mathematicians, and medieval and

Renaissance philosophers,[2] they were more than a

continuation of earlier work. These discoveries not only

added new knowledge, they were the products of innovative

ways of thinking, such as new theories of the nature of

matter and of the universe. The effects of these new ways

of thinking were strongest in the fields of astronomy and

mechanics, where earlier conceptions of the structure of

Transition

the universe underwent a revolution. The principal

developments in these fields were found in the work of

Galileo Galilei in the seventeenth century and Isaac

Newton in the eighteenth.

Early in the seventeenth century, Galileo used the

newly developed telescope to explore the skies and make

observations that proved the Copernican conception of the

solar system was correct.[3] Copernicus believed that the

Evidence

planets revolved around the sun. This challenged the view

of Ptolemy from ancient times, who held that the earth was

the center of the universe.[4] Thus, the Copernican view

relegated the earth to the same status as all other

heavenly bodies. No longer could it be held, as it had

been by all philosophers since Aristotle, that the

movement of earthly objects was completely different from

Evidence

those in space. Galileo's further experiments on moving bodies made clear that we can study objects on earth scientifically just as we can those in space. If

Interpretation

mathematic regularity can be applied to the movement of natural forces on earth as well as to those on other planets, then science could explain acts of nature and answer problems in engineering. This new way of viewing the universe would thus affect a wide range of human concerns.

Evidence

The discoveries of Isaac Newton were even more revolutionary. He developed a mathematical explanation for the motion of all bodies and called it the law of gravitation. This law stated that all matter is mutually attracting. Newton was even able to calculate precisely the intensity of the attraction because he discovered that it depended upon the mass of the bodies and their distance from one another.[5] Now it could clearly be

Interpretation

demonstrated that stars and grains of sand were governed by the same laws. In Newton's view of the universe, the motion of all objects could be explained and even predicted. The universe was a giant machine run by physical laws. This meant that there was no room for

Trans.

religious explanations of how the universe worked. Thus it appeared that the new science would challenge all Greek and Christian thought.

Thematic Dev.

The new developments in astronomy and mechanics established the basis for modern experimental science. In

Evidence

the late seventeenth century, societies for the scientific study of nature grew up in many parts of Europe. Such groups as the Royal Society of London for Promoting

Natural Knowledge spread the new thought and conducted

Interp. experiments.[6] They were part of a new secular outlook that challenged the religious beliefs of Europe. The new and

Transition the old explanations of the world seemed headed for inevitable conflict in their attempts to win the minds of people. What were the essential differences between these two world views and what was the outcome of their struggle?

II. Science versus the Church

Thematic Dev. The new scientific and the old theological views of the universe seemed mutually exclusive. Christianity,

Interpretation through Scripture and other revelation, had an elaborate understanding of the divine origin of the world and of human beings and of the ways in which divine intervention ruled history.[7] Alternative explanations were regarded as the product of ignorance of church teaching or as the work of the devil. On the other hand, science (or natural philosophy as it was then called) held that mathematical logic and tested experience (experimentation) were the only ways to discover truth.[8] Any understanding of the world that was the result of religious experience or church authority was the product of superstition. Newtonian mechanics described a system in which all matter acted according to predictable physical rules. There was no need or even room for God in such a system, and observation and experimentation uncovered no sign of His influence.

The Catholic Church of the seventeenth and eighteenth

Thematic Development

centuries, while it had to share power with secular
rulers, was still strong both theologically and
politically.[9] In many areas it had the power to enforce its
views. The scientists ran great risk if they used their
new ideas and discoveries in ways that threatened
religion.

Evidence

Galileo was prohibited by church authorities in
Rome from writing about or even discussing the religious
implications of the Copernican view of heavenly motions.
Eventually, the Inquisition forced him to renounce the
theory publicly, and his book on the subject, Dialogue on
the Two Chief Systems of the World, was banned.[10]

Thematic Development

The disciplinary authority of the church (and of
those governments influenced by it) was augmented by the
fact that many of the new scientists had been ardent
believers in the Christian faith. Either because they
feared the power of the church and conservative
governments or because they wished, despite their
discoveries, to retain their religious convictions, these

Evidence

scientists sought some kind of theoretical compromise.
Newton, for example, continued to believe in God. While
the operation of his system required no divine presence,
he strongly believed that only God could have been the
creator of such a mechanically perfect universe.[11]

Trans.

As a
result of these factors, the theoretical clash between
science and religion was somewhat muted.

III. The Evolution of Scientific Thought: Deism

Thematic Dev.

One of the most widespread ideas among the new
thinkers was a view that combined the new scientific

Thematic Dev. understanding with a belief, however limited, in God. This idea was known as deism. Deists believed in a "natural religion," one that people arrived at by reason rather

Evid. and Interp. than faith. Since it was not reasonable that the universe created itself, people like John Locke, Samuel Clarke, and John Toland held that God was its creator.[12] While He did not actually intervene once He had set the great machine in motion, God had initially endowed human beings with reason and moral sensibility. By using these faculties, people could learn both to understand nature and to build moral communities.

Thematic Dev. There were, of course, still major differences between Christianity and deism, and the deists were strong critics of the established church. They dispensed with the particulars of orthodox Christianity because these were

Interp. the result not of reason but of superstition. The hierarchy of the church was also unnecessary since if all people could reason, all could come to an understanding of

Trans. God on their own. Nevertheless, deists did believe that the truths uncovered by scientific reasoning were the handiwork of the "Divine Architect."[13]

IV. The Evolution of Scientific Thought: Empiricism

Thematic Dev. Other natural philosophers found the deist compromise unacceptable. These thinkers tended to become agnostics or atheists. Some of these skeptics held that if mechanical

Evid. and Interp. laws explained all things, then they also explained people's belief in God.[14] What believers had taken as miracles, these thinkers explained either as figments of the imagination or else as misunderstood natural phenomena such as earthquakes or lightning. If the evidence of God's presence was unfounded, they held, then there was no reason to assume His existence.

Certain of these skeptics extended the material explanation of things to the workings of the human mind. The philosophy of the British empiricists,[15] in particular, maintained that the mind had no thought content of its own. It merely received sensory information and then made logical connections among the things observed. Since the world is governed by material laws, the impressions that reality makes upon the mind are regular and logical. To perceive truth, all one has to do is observe. If people believe in God, it is because their minds have been filled with superstitious notions that get in the way of understanding the truth as recorded by the senses. This school of empiricism believed that if people were taught to reason from nature rather than from authority, all could come to understand material reality, which was all there was to know.

Empiricism was a radical doctrine because it held that all people were capable of understanding the whole of reality and did not need to depend upon political or religious leaders to guide them. Even more radical were those thinkers who were complete materialists and who not only explained thought as material in origin but also described human beings as just another piece of matter, with no different or higher properties. To these thinkers, if the mind merely registers sensory impressions, then it, too, is nothing more than a machine. Such materialist

philosophers as La Mettrie described people as nothing
more than a material arrangement of bones, muscles, and
nerves.[16] Human thought was merely a particular combination
or arrangement of these material elements. This conception
eliminated not only the need for God but for any system of
morality. As a result, La Mettrie preached hedonism, the
pursuit of pleasure for its own sake, as a completely
acceptable way of life. This view of morality was
supported indirectly by the reports of explorers who
brought home from their scientific expeditions stories
about the unusual social customs of far-off primitive
peoples. The conclusion drawn by many scientifically
minded persons was that morality was culturally taught
and, therefore, relative.

V. The Evolution of Scientific Thought: Skepticism

        Perhaps the end (or rather dead end) of the empirical
school of thought is to be found in the theories of David
Hume. This Scottish skeptic mounted an attack on both
theology and science. He rejected the deist compromise
with its acknowledgment of God as the originator of the
universe. There was no way of knowing, Hume maintained,
that the universe is a machine or that it had to have been
created. These are only inferences derived from the
regularity of its operation. But what evidence do we have
of its regularity? Only the impressions of our senses.
Hume questioned the reliability of sensory impressions,
attacking the foundations of empiricism itself.[17] He argued
that we have no way of being certain that the things we

perceive are real. All we know is the perception itself.
If we cannot know things that are outside our minds, then
the causal connections we make between events (the rising
and setting of the sun, the bouncing ball) are only
habitual connections. Cause and effect is an unprovable
assumption.

VI. The Return toward Nonmaterial Thought

With the new science now as dependent upon faith (in
sensory impressions) as the old religion, the ground was
prepared for a reconciliation. This was accomplished by
the work of Immanuel Kant and Jean Jacques Rousseau.

Kant's Critique of Pure Reason[18] established a new
position from which to view the interaction of mind and
material reality. Kant held that there were two kinds of
mental processes; one kind is observation via the senses,
and the other is a priori. A priori is the innate ability
of the mind to order and reflect upon sensory
impressions. While Kant agreed with Hume that we cannot
know what is outside our minds, he contended that,
because the ability of the mind to organize experience is
consistent and universal, we can be certain that our
thinking is real and that it is understandable to others.
Paradoxically, while we cannot know external reality, we
can know our minds. If the contents of our minds are
real, then all our thought, both rational and spiritual,
is real. Once again, there is room for belief in the
nonmaterial.

It was Rousseau who reintroduced the nonmaterial and,

Thematic Dev.

in a sense, religious element into philosophical thinking.[19] He did so by treating people's sense of right

Evid. and Interp.

and wrong not as the result of religious teaching but as a basic human impulse. He held that the mind could not only reason, it also could feel. People had real emotions—love, hate, fear, pleasure—they were not mental machines. To Rousseau, thinking and feeling were both essential human qualities and were bound to each other.

Evid. and Interp.

Rousseau felt that some of people's strongest feelings were religious ones and that these were not inferior to the reasoning aspect of the mind. Of course, religion for Rousseau was not that of the church with its elaborate rituals or that of the deists to whom God was nothing more than an expert watchmaker. Rousseau's God was present in all natural things, those untouched by the corrupting influence of organized religion or any aspect of modern civilization. Rousseau believed that the human conscience—the least contaminated part of a person—was the best guide to both scientific and moral truth.

Conclusion

Transition

Rousseau brings us to a point where thought is free to trust itself and to be both scientific and moral. Unreasoning faith and faithlessness are both rejected.

Summary

We have seen how the initial clash between science and religion led some scientific thinkers to attempt a synthesis and led others into a godless and eventually purposeless world. Furthermore, we have traced scientific thinking back toward acceptance of nonmaterial,

Interpretation

nonrational ways of thought. Thus the undermining of the Christian world view by scientific thinking was paralleled by an evolution of such thinking itself and in ways that illuminated the enduring strength of moral and religious thought.

Interp. and Conclusion

We have come a long way from the contest between Galileo and the church over the ideas of Copernicus. Today most people combine acceptance of the Copernican universe and much other scientific knowledge with some kind of religious or moral teaching. What seemed in the seventeenth century as a life and death struggle between contradictory ways of thought has turned out to be a standoff and has led to ways of thinking undreamt of by the original antagonists.

The Rough Draft

Here is the rough draft of the concluding section of the preceding paper. This draft is weaker than the final version. Compare the two to see how the language has been strengthened.

Conclusion

Rousseau makes his philosophy both scientific and moral at the same time. He rejects faith and he rejects faithlessness. Now we can see that the original conflict between science and religion led to either a new form of thought or to a godless world. Scientific thinking actually seemed to go backward to less rationalism. The Christian view of the world was undermined, but science never replaced religion.

It was a long road from Galileo's conflict with the church over Copernicus. Most people today agree with

science but they also believe in religion. The seventeenth
century thought that either scientific teaching or moral
teaching was right. It turned out, however, that the
contradictory ways of thought didn't defeat each other but
instead led to new ways of thinking.

Note how the draft has been strengthened in the final version.
The weak phrase "scientific thinking seemed to go backward," is replaced by "we have traced scientific thinking back toward acceptance
of . . ." Thinking *changes* but does not go backward. Another poor
phrase, "The seventeenth century thought that . . ." is replaced since
it is people and not centuries that think. Other changes correct style.
"Now we can see that . . ." becomes "We have seen how . . ." and "It
was a long road from . . ." becomes "We have come a long way
from . . ."

Footnotes: When and How to Use Them

Footnotes give the source of the facts and opinions that appear in
your paper. If you quote, paraphrase, or summarize from your research
materials, you must say where the original information can be found.
This is done so that the reader can check the accuracy of your statements, judge the bias and credibility of your sources, and carry out
research of his or her own. On occasion, you may also want to use
footnotes to make comments that supplement or qualify statements in
your text.

A question that always troubles students is which statements in a
paper need to be footnoted. There are no hard and fast rules concerning the use of footnotes. A professional scholar's criteria will be different from those of a student or amateur researcher. For the student
writing a fifteen- to thirty-page term paper, three types of statements
should be documented: (1) direct quotations, (2) controversial facts or
opinions, and (3) statements that directly support the main points made
in the paper.

All direct quotations must be footnoted. Controversial facts or opinions are those that not all of your sources agree on. If you state that most
slave masters in Mississippi were kind to their slaves, and you know
from your research that there are authors who strongly dispute this, then
you must footnote that statement. A fact or opinion is also controversial if
it is something with which the average reader would disagree. For exam-

ple, you may have found that all your sources agree that Vikings visited the New World long before Columbus. However, if most people believe that Columbus was the first European to see the New World, then it is necessary to show your reader the source of your information with a footnote. Finally, statements of fact or opinion that directly support main points should be footnoted. If your subject is the Protestant Reformation, and you treat nationalism as a major factor in the break with Catholicism, then your references in the text to nationalist forces should be footnoted. On the other hand, if you treat the wealth of the Catholic Church as a very minor factor, then your references to that need not be footnoted.

The number of footnotes to use is another thorny problem. Some papers have more factual or controversial material than others and thus need more footnotes. As a rule of thumb, if your paper has quite a few pages without any footnotes, then you are probably not documenting as much as you should. On the other hand, if you are writing five or more footnotes per page, you may be overdoing it. There is no such thing as the *right* number of footnotes, but a twenty-five-page paper might contain anywhere from fifteen to seventy-five footnotes, depending on the subject.

One final point about what to footnote. Using a footnote does not give you permission to plagiarize. (See Chapter 4, the section on "Avoiding Plagiarism.") You should not use sentences or even phrases from your research sources. Your ideas may come from your sources but the words must be your own.

How to Write Footnotes When you decide that a footnote is necessary, place a number at the end of the sentence that contains the information to be documented. Occasionally, you may want to footnote two different things in the same sentence. In this case, place each number right after the word or phrase you want to footnote. Some writers place the number at the end of a paragraph rather than at the end of a sentence. This is proper only if the footnote refers to the material in the paragraph as a whole. If you are footnoting specific facts or quotations, the number should appear right after the facts or quoted material. If you are footnoting a general idea or opinion, place the number at the end of the paragraph or paragraphs that discuss it. All footnote numbers should be in superscript—that is, a half-line above the line of type. The number should not be put in parentheses and should be inserted after any punctuation (except a dash).

Some writers put their notes at the bottom of the page. This is the form used in many of the books you will use in your research. It is easier for the reader, but it creates problems for the typist, who must judge how much space to leave at the bottom of the page. An easier form, and one that is acceptable to most instructors, is to put all the notes at the end of the paper. If you use this method, you must number your notes consecutively throughout the work and write them on a separate piece of paper as you compose the rough draft. If you know how to use a word-processing program, it can make the job of organizing footnotes much easier. Be sure to learn the commands properly, however, or you may lose your footnotes altogether.

Footnote Form The footnote form illustrated here is a simplified one geared to beginning students.[3] If you have sources that do not fit into these rules, you can check a more advanced manual such as Kate L. Turabian, *Student's Guide for Writing College Papers*. There are two basic forms for writing footnotes, one for books and one for articles:

Books
[1]Crane Brinton, <u>A Decade of Revolution 1789–1799</u> (New York: Harper and Brothers, 1934), pp. 18–22.

1. Author's name in full, followed by a comma.
2. Title in full, underlined.
3. Publication information (enclosed in parentheses and followed by a comma): place of publication, followed by a colon; name of publisher, followed by a comma; date of publication.
4. Page or pages cited, followed by a period.

Some book footnotes are more complex. If a book has several authors, or if it has a translator or editor, or was published in several volumes or editions, then the footnote has to include such information. For example:

[1]T. W. Wallbank and A. M. Taylor, <u>Civilization Past and Present,</u> 2 vols., rev. ed. (Chicago: Scott, Foresman, 1954), 2:12, 104–117.

---

[3]Check to see if your instructor prefers a different form. Some do not require publication information in footnotes. Others permit the use of the social science system of notation, which is different from the one described here.

Note that when there are two authors, both are listed. If there are more than three authors, the footnote includes the name of the one listed first in the book followed by "et al." ("and others"). If there is more than one volume to a work, the total number of volumes must be specified and inserted after the title. The number of the specific volume used is placed before the page numbers and is separated from them by a colon. If the particular book used is a later edition of the work, that too is inserted after the title. Note also from the example that pages from two different parts of the same book can be covered in one footnote. If there is an editor or translator, that person's name, followed by "ed." or "trans.," appears in the place reserved for the author's name:

> ¹Eugene C. Black, ed., Posture of Europe 1815–1940 (Homewood, Ill.: Dorsey Press, 1964), p. 102.

Articles
> ¹Dana F. Fleming, "The Role of the Senate in Treaty Making," American Political Science Review, XXVIII (August 1934), p. 583.

1. Author's name in full, followed by a comma.
2. Title of article, followed by a comma, all in quotation marks.
3. Title of periodical (journal or magazine), underlined and followed by a comma.
4. Volume number in either Roman (XIV) or Arabic (vol. 14) numerals, date in parentheses, followed by a comma.
5. Page or pages cited, followed by a period.

If the article is an editorial or has no author, the footnote begins with the name of the article:

> ¹"America's Interest in the Cuban Economy," Barrons, XVI (January 20, 1936), p. 9.

This form is common for popular magazines, editorials, and many newspaper articles.

For specialized sources such as unpublished materials, book reviews, microfilm, speeches, dissertations, interviews, government documents, private correspondence, and radio or television programs, see a more specialized book, such as Turabian.⁴

---

⁴For a common list of abbreviations used in footnotes, see Appendix B.

A final rule about footnotes regards *second references* to the same source. If you refer to a particular book or article in more than one footnote, only the first reference has to have all of the information. The second reference to the same book need include only the author's last name and the page number.[5] If your first footnote read

> [1]Robert F. Kennedy, Thirteen Days (New York: W. W. Norton & Co., 1969), p. 14.

your second and later references would read simply

> [7]Kennedy, p. 123.
> [12]Kennedy, p. 168.

If, however, you are also referring to other books or articles by Robert Kennedy, you will have to repeat the title so that your reader knows to which material you are referring.

The second time you refer to an article, you need to repeat only the name of the author and the page.[6] Thus if your first footnote to an article read

> [1]Julius W. Pratt, "American Business and the Spanish-American War," Hispanic American Historical Review, XIV (May 1934), pp. 184–187.

your second and later references would read simply

> [4]Pratt, pp. 189–191.

Again, if you are also referring to another article or book by Pratt, later references will have to include the name of the book or article.

Whenever you write a footnote, ask yourself: is it clear to the reader exactly which source I am referring to, and does that reader have enough information to find that source if necessary?

Here is a sample series of footnotes illustrating the various rules discussed above:

> [1]Charles Stanforth, *The Study of History* (New York: Crown, 1961), pp. 42, 122–127.

---

[5]Some instructors prefer second references to include a shortened title as well as the author's last name and the page number.

[6]See footnote 5.

²Cleveland Roland, "Machiavelli and Modern History," *Journal of the Philosophy of History*, XIV (February 1949), p. 49.

³*Encyclopedia of Historical Science*, 2nd ed., "Whig Interpretation of History," by Rudolph Klein.

⁴*Encyclopedia of Historical Science*, "Calvinism," by Nancy Ring Brenner.

⁵Charles Stanforth, *Cyclical Theory in Arnold Toynbee* (London: Greath & Sons, 1950), p. 42. This view is also held, though less dogmatically, by Norman Parton, *Ancient and Modern Thinking* (London: Fernival & Ashwood, 1956), pp. 98–106.

⁶"Historians at War Again," *Los Angeles Dispatch*, January 14, 1969, sec. B, p. 2.

⁷Michelle Arnold and Dana Swope, eds., *New Trends in Historiography* (Philadelphia: Claxton, 1972), p. 104.

⁸Stanforth, *Cyclical Theory*, p. 14.

⁹Roland, p. 50.

Explanation of footnote citations:

Footnote 1: Book; first citation.

2: Article; first citation.

3: Reference work. Author and publisher not needed; edition or date of publication is needed; title and author (if mentioned) of article consulted; volume and page number not needed because of alphabetical arrangement of work.

4: Reference work; second citation but to different article.

5: Book, first citation (even though author was previously mentioned in footnote 1). Note that you can refer to more than one source in a footnote as long as you explain your reason for doing so.

6: Newspaper article.

7: Book; multiple authors or editors.

8: Book; second citation. Short title needed because two different works by this author were previously cited.

9: Article; second citation. No short title needed because no other work by this author is cited.

Quotations

Don't quote too often, and don't make quotations too long. Many students tend to rely on other people's words more than necessary.

What to Quote Unless the exact words of your source are crucial to making an important point, or unless great controversy surrounds the statement, it is not necessary to use a quotation. In most cases a paraphrase or summary of the statement, properly footnoted, is sufficient. If you do quote, be sure to quote enough of the original statement to make its meaning clear, but do not make the quotations any longer than necessary. Remember that a quotation must clearly be labeled as such and the speaker clearly identified.

Quotation Form If a quotation is brief, taking up no more than two or three lines of your paper, then it should be written as a part of the text and surrounded by quotation marks. You should introduce the quotation by clearly identifying the speaker. The reader will always want to know who is speaking and in what context. Don't say: *The strikers were "a dangerous mob."* Say: *According to D. H. Dyson, the plant manager, the strikers were "a dangerous mob."* If you do not wish to quote a whole statement, it is necessary to indicate those parts that you are leaving out by inserting ellipses (three periods " . . .") wherever words are missing. (See the example that follows.)

If your quotation is very long, it must be separated from the sentences that precede and follow it. It should be indented ten or more spaces and appear in single-spaced type. Do not surround it with quotation marks.

Short quotation example:
The early settlers were not hostile to the native Americans. As pointed out by the Claxton Banner in 1836: "Our Sioux neighbors, despite their fierce reputation, are a friendly and peaceable people."

Short quotation example with omission:
As pointed out by the Claxton Banner in 1836: "Our Sioux neighbors . . . are a friendly and peaceable people."

Long quotation example:
The early settlers were not hostile to the native Americans. As pointed out by the Claxton Banner in 1836:
Our Sioux neighbors, despite their fierce reputation, are a friendly and peaceable people. No livestock have been disturbed, and the outermost cabins are unmolested. We trust in God that our two peoples may live in harmony in this territory.

It is also possible to insert quoted material in the middle of a sentence (for example, *the Prime Minister favored the proposal, but the Foreign Secretary felt it to be "a most dangerous course to pursue," and urged its rejection*). In most cases like this, however, a paraphrase is preferable to a quotation. (*The Prime Minister favored the proposal, but the Foreign Secretary considered it dangerous and urged its rejection.*) Whether you choose to quote or paraphrase, all such references must be footnoted.[7]

Organizing a Bibliography

A bibliography is an alphabetical listing of the sources you used in writing your paper.[8] The list should appear on a separate page or pages at the end of the paper. If the bibliography is long, say more than twenty sources, it should be divided into three categories: (1) primary sources and documents, (2) books, and (3) articles. The sources are listed alphabetically according to the last name of the author.

The form for books is

> Link, Arthur S. Woodrow Wilson and the Progressive Era. New York: Harper & Row, 1954.
> 1. Author, last name first, followed by a period.
> 2. Title of work, underlined, followed by a period.
> 3. Place of publication, followed by a colon.
> 4. Publisher, followed by a comma.
> 5. Date of publication, followed by a period.

The form for articles is

> Bettman, Irwin. "The Beet Sugar Industry: A Study in Tariff Protection." Harvard Business Review. XI (April 1933), pp. 369–378.
> 1. Author, last name first, followed by a period.
> 2. Title of article, followed by a period, all in quotation marks.
> 3. Name of the periodical, underlined, followed by a period.

---

[7]If a portion of the material you are quoting is in italics (e.g., *New York Times*), you should underline these words when you type them (e.g., New York Times). This is not necessary, however, if your word-processing program allows you to italicize.

[8]It must include all those sources that appear in footnotes. You need not list every source you looked at in the course of your research. Don't pad the bibliography just to make it look more impressive.

4. Volume number, followed by date in parentheses, followed by a comma.
5. Pages on which the article begins and ends, followed by a period.

If there is more than one author, the citation is alphabetized according to the last name of the first author mentioned on the title page of the work. That name is then followed by *all* the others, again with last names first. If there is more than one work by a particular author, only the first listing in the bibliography carries the author's name. All the rest begin with an eight-space underline in place of the name. As with footnotes, if the author is the translator or editor, or if there is more than one volume, these must be noted. If a book is anonymous, it is listed in alphabetical order by its title. If an article has no author, it is listed, in alphabetical order, by the title of the article. If you have used many volumes of a particular periodical or many issues of a particular newspaper, you need not list each one separately in your bibliography. They should appear, listed by the name of the periodical or newspaper, as follows:

Monthly Labor Review. Vols. XL–LXX. Washington: United States Bureau of Labor Statistics, 1940–1957.

New York Times. 1954–1958.

The rules governing bibliographical citations for primary documents can be complicated. The best system is to copy the information exactly as it appears in the card catalog.

Here is a sample bibliography illustrating the rules discussed above. It is drawn from the series of footnotes appearing on page 102. Note that in the footnote series the first line was indented, while in the bibliography it is the second and subsequent lines that are indented.

Arnold, Michelle and Swope, Dana, eds. *New Trends in Historiography*. Philadelphia: Claxton, 1972.

Encyclopedia of Historical Science, 2nd ed. "Calvinism" by Nancy Ring Brenner.

————. "Whig Interpretation of History" by Rudolph Klein.

"Historians at War Again." *Los Angeles Dispatch*, January 14, 1969.

Parton, Norman. *Ancient and Modern Thinking*. London: Fernival & Ashwood, 1956.

Roland, Cleveland. "Machiavelli and Modern History."
Journal of the Philosophy of History. XIV (February
1949), 46–60.
Stanforth, Charles. *Cyclical Theory in Arnold Toynbee.*
London: Greath & Sons, 1950.
————. *The Study of History.* New York: Crown, 1961.

Revising and Rewriting

Leave time for revising your paper. The process of putting together the research and writing of a history paper is complex, and your first draft will need smoothing out. As you prepare the final draft, check your paper for the following: (1) Does the paper have thematic unity and do its parts follow one from the other? (2) Is there adequate support for the major assertions of fact and interpretation? (3) Are the points made clearly and forcefully? You must also check the mechanics of your paper, especially spelling and grammar. If your paper is typewritten, check for typographical errors, and make all corrections cleanly and clearly. Reading the paper aloud will help you to catch poor sentence construction and awkward phrases.

Preparing your final draft involves knowledge of the rules of typing style. Make sure that all pages are numbered consecutively, that the sections or chapters are clearly delineated, and that the footnotes and bibliography are clearly separated from the text and neatly organized. If your paper contains additional material such as appendices, graphs, charts, drawings, photographs, or maps, these too must be clearly labeled and separated from the text. If there are many such materials, your paper should contain a table of contents that lists them. Last of all, choose a title for your paper—one that clearly and accurately reflects its contents.

Word Processing

If you have not already learned to use a word-processing program, it is important that you do so. Most schools make computers available to students who are preparing papers. Computers make the typing, and especially the revising, of papers a far easier task.

The most important rule about word processing is "Know your program!" This includes becoming familiar with the particular computer you are using. Work with the program and the computer until you are at home with all of its features—its peculiarities as well as its power. Using a program you are not familiar with can lead to problems. It is unlikely, but an incorrect command may cause you to lose everything you have written. Be sure to "save" your work periodically to reduce this risk.

There is no substitute for thorough knowledge of the hardware and software with which you are working.

Whatever word-processing program you may use, there are a few simple rules of style for research papers. Leave at least a one-inch margin on all sides. Double-space your text except for long quotations and footnotes. Give each page a consecutive number. Prepare a separate title page that includes your name and identifies the course and instructor. Check with your instructor for more specific directions.

Basic Reference Sources
for History Study
and Research

This appendix should be used to begin your exploration of the reference collection of your school library.[1] To aid you in your research, the sources are separated according to the kind of information they contain, and, where appropriate, they are organized according to area or subject. This should be particularly valuable in locating sources as you begin your study of a particular subject. If you have no initial leads on relevant material, or if you are unsatisfied with the sources you have uncovered, the works listed here may enable you to find pertinent facts and historical works.

The reference sources cited here are especially designed for historical

[1]For information on how to use reference sources in the library, see pages 65–67.

research. Two kinds of works are listed: reference books, which contain summary or statistical historical information, and bibliographies, which contain lists of historical works on particular periods or subjects. Reference books (dictionaries, encyclopedias, biography collections, etc.) are useful for obtaining specific facts or for organizing a general outline of your subject. Bibliographies do not themselves contain historical information but rather are collections of history works on a particular topic.

The purpose of this appendix is to facilitate your search for relevant historical facts and history books. Because it is organized with the needs of the beginning student in mind, it may be easier to use than the catalogs in your school library. It is therefore a good place to *begin* your research. However, as stated before, it is meant as a *supplement* rather than as a substitute for your library's catalogs. Many of the works cited here should be available in a good college or public library, but some, particularly the specialized bibliographies, may not be. If a book is listed here that you believe is valuable for your research but it is not in your library's collection, try another library or find a comparable work that your library does possess. On the other hand, if your library is large, its reference catalog will have many more sources than are listed in this appendix, and you should treat these listings as only a first step in your research.

Within each group of sources, those that should be found in most library reference collections or that are particularly useful to beginning students are designated by an asterisk (*). Works without an asterisk are less likely to be available at smaller libraries and are generally designed for the use of advanced students and professionals. If any of the latter should be available, however, you should find them valuable in your research.

The books in this appendix are listed by title first so that you can easily sight the volume that seems closest to your topic. Following the title is the publication information and then the name of the editor or compiler. When looking up one of these works in a catalog, check first under the name of the editor or compiler. If the book is not listed there, it may be filed under the title of the work or possibly the publisher. When there is more than one edition of a work, use the most recent. In many instances the librarian will be able to locate the reference book by its title alone.

I. Dictionaries, Encyclopedias, Atlases, and Yearbooks

Dictionaries, encyclopedias, atlases, yearbooks, and so on, are general reference works. They can help you to define and correctly spell important terms, gather general information on a particular subject, locate geographical areas, obtain statistical data, and much more. These sources are a good point at which to begin any historical investigation. You can also consult them for specific facts. However, these sources do not contain serious developments or interpretations of historical subjects, and therefore you should not depend upon them for the substance of your work.

A. General Dictionaries

Oxford English Dictionary. Oxford: Clarendon Press, 1888–1920. James A. H. Murray et al., eds. *Supplement* 1972, 1976, and 1982, R. W. Birchfield, ed.
This is the most complete English-language dictionary. If you are studying the historical development of the meaning of a word, it is an essential reference. If, however, you wish to determine the contemporary spelling or definition of a term, the following unabridged language dictionaries are better sources. If the term is colloquial or is a recent derivation, be sure to use the most recent edition available.
*Webster's New International Dictionary
*Funk and Wagnall's New Standard Dictionary
*The Random House Dictionary of the American Language

B. Historical Dictionaries

Historical dictionaries define only historical terms. Unlike language dictionaries, they briefly describe the origin and general historical context of the term. Some historical dictionaries give extensive explanations of terms and thus are similar to encyclopedias.

*Webster's Guide to American History. Springfield, Mass.: G. and C. Merriam, 1971.
*Concise Dictionary of American History. New York: Charles Scribner's Sons, 1983. David William Voorhees, ed. This is an abridgement of the eight-volume *Dictionary of American History.*
Dictionary of American History. New York: Scribner's, 1942–1961. James T. Adams and Roy V. Coleman, eds. (Revised edition, 1976.) This is the most extensive dictionary of American history.
The Almanac of American History. New York: Putnam Publishing Group, 1984. Arthur M. Schlesinger, Jr., ed.
The Harper Dictionary of Modern Thought. New York: Harper & Row, 1988. Alan Bullock and Stephen Trombley, eds.

Macmillan Concise Dictionary of World History. New York: Macmillan, 1983. Bruce Wetterau, comp. and ed.

An Encyclopedic Dictionary of American History. New York: Washington Square Press, 1974. Howard Hurwitz, ed.

Concise Dictionary of Ancient History. New York: Philosophical Society, 1955. Percival Woodcock, ed.

*A Dictionary of Twentieth Century History, 1914–1990. Oxford: Oxford University Press, 1992. Peter Teed, ed.

*A Dictionary of Modern History, 1789–1945. Baltimore: Penguin Books, 1975. Alan W. Palmer, ed.

C. Specialized Dictionaries

A Dictionary of the Social Sciences. New York: The Free Press, 1964. J. Gould and W. Kolb, eds.

The New Grove Dictionary of Music and Musicians. New York: Macmillan, 1980. Stanley Sadie, ed. 20v.

D. General Encyclopedias

If your subject is a recent one, or if important new facts and interpretations have arisen in recent years, be sure to obtain the latest edition of whatever encyclopedia you use. If a recent edition is not available, check the annual supplements published by most good encyclopedias.

*Encyclopaedia Britannica. Chicago: Encyclopaedia Britannica Educational Corporation. This is one of the best encyclopedias.

*Encyclopedia Americana. Danbury, Conn.: Grolier Educational Corporation.

*Collier's Encyclopedia. New York: Crowell Collier and Macmillan.

The Columbia Encyclopedia. New York: Columbia University Press.

E. Historical Encyclopedias

*An Encyclopedia of World History, Ancient, Medieval and Modern, Chronologically Arranged. Boston: Houghton Mifflin, 1972. William L. Langer, ed.

*Harper Encyclopedia of the Modern World [1760 to present]. New York: Harper & Row, 1970. Richard B. Morris and Graham W. Irwin, eds.

*Encyclopedia of American History. New York: Harper & Row, 1982. Richard B. Morris et al., eds.

Encyclopedia of American Political History: Studies of the Principal Movements and Ideas. New York: Scribner's, 1984. Jack P. Green, ed. 3v.

Women's Studies Encyclopedia: History, Philosophy, and Religion. Vol. III. Westport, Conn.: Greenwood Press, 1991. Helen Tierney, ed.

F. Specialized Encyclopedias

*International Encyclopedia of the Social Sciences. New York: Free Press, 1977. David L. Sills, ed. If your research takes you into such fields as political science, economics, anthropology, law, sociology, and psychology, this is an important sourcebook for you. (A biographical supplement, published in 1979, includes biographies of famous social scientists.) An earlier work, Encyclopedia of the Social Sciences (New York: Macmillan, 1930–1934), edited by Edwin R. A. Seligman and Alvin Johnson, is also valuable for such subjects, although it is now out of date.

Encyclopedia of Philosophy. New York: Free Press, 1973. Paul Edwards, ed.

Encyclopedia Judaica. Jerusalem: Keter Publishing House, 1972. Geofrey Wigoder, ed. 16v.

New Catholic Encyclopedia. Palantine, Ill.: J. Heraty, 1981.

Encyclopedia of Religion. New York: Macmillan, 1987. Mircea Eliade, ed. 16v.

The Cambridge History of Islam. New York: Cambridge University Press, 1970. P. M. Holt, et al., eds.

Encyclopedia of World Art. New York: McGraw Hill, 1959–1968. Supplements, 1987.

Benets' Readers Encyclopedia of American Literature. New York: Harper Collins, 1991. George Perkins, ed.

The Concise Encyclopedia of Islam. New York: Harper & Row, 1989. Cyril Glasse, ed.

G. General Atlases

The Times Atlas of the World. London: Times Publishing Company, 1955–1959. John Bartholomew, ed. Vol. I—World, Australia, East Asia; Vol. II—India, Middle East, Russia; Vol. III—Northern Europe; Vol. IV—Mediterranean and Africa; Vol. V—Americas. A one-volume edition was published in 1985.

Oxford Economic Atlas of the World. Oxford: Oxford University Press, 1972.

*Webster's New Geographical Dictionary. Springfield Mass.: G. and C. Merriam, 1984. Although this source is not useful for map reference, it is a convenient source for determining the spelling, location, and description of geographical terms.

Oxford World Atlas. New York: Oxford University Press, 1973.
National Geographic Atlas of the World. Washington, D.C.: National
   Geographic Society, 1981.

H. Historical Atlases

The Times Concise Atlas of World History. Maplewood, N.J.: Ham-
   mond, 1984. Geoffrey Barraclough, ed.
Rand McNally Historical Atlas of the World. Chicago: Rand McNally,
   1981. R. I. Moore, gen. ed.
Historical Atlas of the Religions of the World. New York: Macmillan,
   1974. Ismail Ragi al Faruqi, ed.
The Atlas of Medieval Man. New York: Crescent Books, 1985. Colin
   Platt, ed.
Shepherd's Historical Atlas. New York: Harper & Row, 1980. William R.
   Shepherd, ed.
Atlas of American History. New York: Scribner's, 1984. Kenneth T.
   Jackson, ed.
Historical Atlas of the United States. Washington D.C.: National Geo-
   graphic Society, 1988. Wilbur E. Garrett, ed.
Historical Atlas of Britain. New York: Continuum, 1981. Malcolm
   Falkus, ed.
Muir's Atlas of Ancient and Classical History. London: George Philips,
   1982.
Muir's Historical Atlas: Ancient, Medieval & Modern. London: George
   Philips, 1976.
Atlas of World History. Chicago: Rand McNally, 1975. Robert R. Palmer
   et al., eds.
Atlas of the Greek World. New York: Facts on File, 1982. Peter Levi,
   comp.
Atlas of the Roman World. New York: Facts on File, 1982. Tim Cornell
   and John Matthews, comps.
Atlas of Industrializing Britain, 1780–1914. London: Methuen, 1985.
   John Langton and R. J. Morris, eds.

I. Yearbooks

Statesman's Yearbook. New York: St. Martin's Press, 1864–present.
   This and the following yearbooks provide up-to-date political infor-
   mation, especially of a governmental nature.
Political Handbook of the World. New York: McGraw-Hill, 1927–
   present. Arthur S. Banks and William Overstreet, eds.
United Nations Statistical Yearbook. New York: United Nations Statisti-

cal Office, 1949–present. There is also a *United Nations Demographic Yearbook,* which provides world and national population statistics.

II. Biography Collections

Biography collections consist of short biographies of well-known persons. They contain a general outline of the milestones and accomplishments of individuals who have made notable contributions to the times in which they lived and/or to posterity. These works are useful as a first step in biographical research on persons central to your topic or as a way of identifying characters peripheral to it. Each collection has different criteria for determining which individuals it includes. Take care to select the biography collection that is most likely to include the type of individual on whom you are seeking information.

A. Guides to Biography Collections

Biography Index: A Cumulative Guide to Biographical Material in Books and Magazines. New York: H. W. Wilson, 1949–present.

Biography and Genealogy Master Index. Detroit: Gale, 1980. Miranda C. Herbert and Barbara McNeil, eds. 8v. Supplements issued in 1981/82, 1983, 1984, 1985.

Biographical Dictionaries Master Index. Detroit: Gale, 1975–. Dennis La Beau and Gary C. Tarbert, eds.

B. British and Canadian Biography Collections

Dictionary of National Biography. Oxford: Oxford University Press, 1908–present. Leslie Stephen and Sidney Lee, eds. A summary of this large multivolume collection can be found in *A Concise Dictionary of National Biography,* vol. 1, to 1900; vol. 2, 1901–1970.

Who's Who. London: Allen & Unwin, 1849–present. Annual. This volume covers *living* individuals. For historical research, you must choose a year during which your subject was most active, or preferably use the *Who Was Who* collection that follows.

Who Was Who. Vol. I, 1897–1915; Vol. II, 1916–1928; Vol. III, 1929–1940; Vol. IV, 1941–1950; Vol. V, 1951–1960; Vol. VI, 1961–1970; Vol. VII, 1971–1980. A cumulative index for 1897–1980 was published in 1981. (See annotation to *Who Was Who in America* for further information.)

Canadian Who's Who. Toronto: University of Toronto Press, 1984, 19v.

Dictionary of Canadian Biography. Toronto: University of Toronto Press, 1966–present. An index to this multivolume work is listed below.

Dictionary of Canadian Biography: Index. Volumes I to XII, 1000 to 1900. Toronto: University of Toronto Press, 1991.
The Macmillan Dictionary of Canadian Biography. New York: Macmillan of Canada, 1978. W. Stewart Wallace, ed.

C. American Biography Collections

*Dictionary of American Biography. New York: Scribner's, 1928–1958, including supplements. This is the best source for biographies of historical personages of the United States. It includes both American citizens and people who lived much of their lives in this country even if they were not citizens. It lists only individuals who are no longer living. As with most biography collections, the date of original publication is the best key to determining who is included. Most of the original volumes were written between 1928 and 1936. If your subject died after 1928, check the supplements. Supplements cover deaths through the following years: I, 1935; II, 1940; III, 1945; IV, 1950; V, 1955; VI, 1960; VII, 1965. A one-volume work containing shortened versions of these biographies is published under the title *Concise Dictionary of American Biography,* 3rd ed., 1980.
National Cyclopedia of American Biography. Ann Arbor, Mich.: University Microfilms, 1967. Unlike the *Dictionary of American Biography,* this is not an alphabetical listing, but it does have an alphabetical index at the end of each volume. This collection is published in two series: a "Current" series and a "Permanent" series. The Permanent series includes only individuals no longer living at date of publication for the volume in which they were to be included. Although this work was reprinted in 1967, the original volumes of the Permanent series were written in the 1890s. If your subject was living in the twentieth century, consult the Current series, which includes only persons living at date of publication. A cumulative index to both the Permanent and Current series has been published by J. T. White and Co., 1984.
Who's Who in America. Chicago: Marquis Who's Who, 1897–present. This volume covers living individuals. For purposes of historical research, you must obtain the older volumes or, preferably, use the *Who Was Who* collections that follow.
Who Was Who in America. Vol. I, 1897–1942; Vol. II, 1943–1950; Vol. III, 1951–1960; Vol. IV, 1961–1968; Vol. V, 1969–1973; Vol. VI, 1974–1976; Vol. VII, 1977–1981; Vol. VIII, 1982–1985. Chicago: Marquis Who's Who. The years covered in each volume indicate

the dates of death for those included in it. For example, if your subject died in 1945, he or she should be included in Volume II. For individuals who died before 1897, see the following citation.

Who Was Who in America: Historical Volume, 1607–1896. Chicago: Marquis Who's Who, 1967. If you are uncertain about your subject's death date, check *Who Was Who Index, 1607–1981.*

Research Guide to American Historical Biography. New York: Beacham, 1988. Robert Muccigrosso, ed.

Biographical Directory of the American Congress, 1774–1989. Washington, D.C.: Government Printing Office, 1989.

Biographical Directory of the United States Executive Branch, 1774–1989. Westport, Conn.: Greenwood Press, 1990.

Who's Who of American Women. Chicago: Marquis Who's Who, 1958–.

Notable American Women 1607–1950: A Bibliographical Dictionary. Cambridge, Mass.: Harvard University Press, 1971. Edward T. James, ed. 3v. Supplemented by: *Notable American Women: The Modern Period.* 1980. This volume includes women who died from 1951 through 1975.

Dictionary of American Negro Biography. New York: W. W. Norton, 1982. Rayford W. Logan and Michael Winston, eds.

Biographical Directory of American Labor. Westport, Conn.: Greenwood Press, 1984. Gary M. Fink, ed.

A Bibliography of American Autobiographies. Madison: University of Wisconsin Press, 1961. Louis Kaplan et al., comps.

American Autobiography, 1945–1980: A Bibliography. Madison: University of Wisconsin Press, 1982.

American Men and Women of Science. New York: Bowker, 1906–present.

Directory of American Scholars. New York: Bowker. American Council of Learned Societies. NY: R. R. Bowker, 1982.

D. International Biography Collections

International biography collections list persons of all national origins.

Current Biography. New York: H. W. Wilson, 1940–present. This covers living persons. Older volumes, however, may list individuals who are now of historical significance. Only useful for historical research for the period since the 1930s. To locate the volume you need, check *Current Biography: Cumulated Index, 1940–1970.*

International Who's Who. London: Europa, 1935–present.

New York Times Obituary Index, 1858–1968, 1969–1980. New York: New York Times, 1970, 1980.
Encyclopedia of World Biography. New York, McGraw-Hill, 1973. David I. Eggenberger, ed.
Obituaries: A Guide to Sources. Boston: G. K. Hall and Company, 1982. Betty M. Jarboe.
Who's Who in the World. Chicago: Marquis, 1971–Present.
The International Dictionary of Women's Biography. New York: Continuum, 1982. Jennifer S. Uglow, ed.
Makers of Nineteenth-Century Culture, 1800–1914. London: Routledge & Kegan Paul, 1982. Justin Wintle, ed.
Makers of Modern Culture. New York: Facts on File, 1981. Justin Wintle, ed.
Chambers's Biographical Dictionary. Edison, N.J.: Two Continents, 1978. J. O. Thorne and T. C. Collocott, eds.
Biographical Directory of Modern Peace Leaders. Westport, Conn.: Greenwood Press, 1985. Harold Josephson, ed.-in-chief.

E. National Biography Collections

Most national biography collections, except for those of the United Kingdom and the United States, which are covered separately, deal with contemporary personages. However, such collections may be useful for research into recent history or for obtaining information on the early careers of contemporary figures. Here is a brief selection.

Dictionary of Canadian Biography. Toronto: University of Toronto Press, 1966–present.
Who's Who in Latin America. Chicago: A. N. Marquis, 1946–1951. Percy A. Martin, ed.
Dictionary of African Historical Biography. Berkeley, CA: University of California Press, 1986. Mark R. Lipschultz and R. Kent Rasmusson, eds.
Who's Who in Communist China. Hong Kong: Union Research Institute, 1966.
Who's Who in the Union of Soviet Socialist Republics. New York: Scarecrow Press, 1966.
Dictionary of African Biography. New York: Reference Publications, 1977–present. Volumes expected on each African country.
South African Dictionary of National Biography. London: Warne, 1966. Eric Rosenthal, ed.

Japan Biographical Encyclopedia and Who's Who. Tokyo: Rengo Press, 1958–present.

Biographical Dictionary of Republican China. New York: Columbia University Press, 1967–1979.

Australian Dictionary of Biography, 1788–1939. Carlton, Victoria: Melbourne University Press, 1966–1983. Bede Nairn and Geoffrey Serle, eds. 9v.

F. Specialized Biography Collections

A Biographical Dictionary of World War II. New York: St. Martin's Press, 1972. Christopher Tunney, ed.

Biographical Dictionary of World War I. Westport, Conn.: Greenwood Press, 1982. Holger H. Herwig and Heil M. Heyman, eds.

Biographical Encyclopedia of Science and Technology. Garden City, N.Y.: Doubleday, 1982. Isaac Asimov, ed.

Dictionary of Scientific Biography. New York: Scribner's, 1970–1980. Charles C. Gillispie, ed. 16v., includes index.

Who's Who in Jewish History: After the Period of the Old Testament. New York: McKay, 1974. Joan Comay, ed.

III. Newspaper Directories and Indexes

In most cases, the beginning student will have access only to the few newspapers held in the school or local public library. If you determine, however, that a particular newspaper is especially important to you, the best way to locate back issues is to check a newspaper directory. These directories can tell you in which libraries that newspaper can be found and how complete the collection is. Remember, the newspaper directory is useful only if you know the name of the paper for which you are looking. Moreover, unless you have easy access to a large university or public library, most of the newspapers in a directory will be located far from your school. You might be able to obtain the newspapers you need if they are on microfilm or microfiche, but this can take several weeks. In most cases, it is best to limit yourself to the newspaper collections in nearby libraries.

A. Newspaper Directories

American Newspapers, 1821–1936: A Union List of Files Available in the United States and Canada. New York: H. W. Wilson, 1937. Winifred Gerould, ed. Also available on microfilm. Ann Arbor: University Microfilms, 1966.

Newspapers on Microfilm: A Union Check List. Washington, D.C.: Library of Congress, 1963. George Schwegman, Jr., ed. This volume is supplemented by *Newspapers in Microform: United States, 1948–1984.*

African Newspapers in Selected American Libraries. Washington, D.C.: Library of Congress, 1965.

Latin American Newspapers in United States Libraries. Austin: University of Texas Press, 1969. Steven M. Charno, ed.

B. Newspaper Indexes

Once you have access to a particular newspaper, you must determine which issues contain articles on your subject. If your subject is a specific event, then merely check the issues of the newspaper published at the time of or shortly after the event. However, if you are seeking articles about an event that was not confined to a particular day or week (for example, the stock market crash of 1929), then you will have to check newspaper issues covering many weeks or even months. An indispensable aid in such a task is the newspaper index.

If you know the year in which the event occurred, then a newspaper index can tell you the days in that year when a particular paper contained related articles or editorials. The only problem with newspaper indexes is that so few of them exist. If there is no index to the paper you wish to read, check the index of another newspaper. This will tell you the dates on which that newspaper carried articles on your subject. You can then go back to the newspaper in which you were initially interested and read it for those dates. In most cases, you will find what you need.

*New York Times Index. New York: New York Times, 1913–present. This is usually the best source for beginning students. Most libraries have files of the *New York Times,* and the index has been extended back to 1851.

New York Daily Tribune Index. New York: Tribune Association, 1841–1907.

Palmer's Index to The Times [of London] *Newspaper,* 1790–1941. London: 1868–1943.

Official Index to The Times [of London]. London: 1907–present.

Christian Science Monitor Index. Corvallis, Oregon: 1960–present. Because this index goes back only to 1960, it is of limited use for historical research.

IV. Periodical Guides and Indexes

Periodical guides describe the location and general content of periodicals. Like newspaper guides, they are most useful if you already know which periodical you need and want to find out where collections of it are located. If the periodical guide lists no library convenient to you, it is best to check into other periodicals.

A. Periodical Guides

Union List of Serials in Libraries of the United States and Canada. New York: H. W. Wilson, 1943.

New Serial Titles: A Union List of Serials Commencing Publication after December 31, 1949. Washington, D.C.: Library of Congress, 1953–present. If you are seeking a newer periodical, this guide is the best source.

Historical Periodicals: An Annotated World List of Historical and Related Serial Publications. Santa Barbara, Cal.: ABC-Clio, 1961. Eric H. Boehm and Lalit Adolphus, eds. This volume is brought up to date by the directory that follows.

Historical Periodicals Directory. Vol. I, United States and Canada, 1981; Vol. II, Europe (West), 1982; Vol. III, Europe (East), 1982; Vol. IV, Africa, Asia, and Latin America, 1983. Santa Barbara, Cal.: ABC-Clio. Eric H. Boehm, Barbara H. Pope, and Marie Ensign, eds.

Ulrich's International Periodicals Directory. New York: R.R. Bowker, 1985.

B. General Periodical Indexes

General periodical indexes list articles that have appeared in periodical publications. Usually organized by subject, they contain all of the articles on a given topic that appeared in the periodicals that are indexed. The periodicals covered by a particular index are usually listed at the beginning of the volume. When you choose an index, be sure that it covers the kind of periodical likely to contain articles on your subject and that these articles are written for a serious or scholarly audience. There are also several databases that index periodicals. (See Appendix A, section XI.)

Historical Abstracts. Santa Barbara, Cal.: ABC-Clio, 1955–present. Part A: Modern History (1450–1914); Part B: The Twentieth Century (1914–present). Eric H. Boehm, ed. This is the best source for articles in history journals. It covers a wide range of subjects. A brief description of each article is included. After 1964, it does not include articles on United States or Canadian history. Also available in database form.

America: History and Life: A Guide to Periodical Literature. Santa Barbara, Cal.: ABC-Clio, 1965–present. Supplement, 1980. A brief description of each article is included. It covers the United States and Canada. Also available in database form.

Reader's Guide to Periodical Literature. New York: H. W. Wilson, 1900–present. These volumes cover the twentieth century. Be selective when using them because many of the periodicals included are written for a popular rather than a scholarly audience. However, the magazines listed are valuable as records of popular opinions and interests.

Nineteenth Century Reader's Guide to Periodical Literature. New York: H. W. Wilson, 1944.

Poole's Index to Periodical Literature, 1802–1881. Boston: Houghton Mifflin, 1891. There is a supplement covering 1882–1906.

Social Science and Humanities Index. New York: H. W. Wilson, 1907– 1973. This is often the best single guide for historical researchers.

Social Sciences Index. New York: H. W. Wilson, 1974–present. For the period prior to 1974, see *Social Science and Humanities Index.*

Humanities Index. New York: H. W. Wilson, 1974–present. For the period prior to 1974, see *Social Science and Humanities Index.*

Public Affairs Information Service Bulletin. New York: P.A.I.S., 1915– present. This work emphasizes periodicals and other publications in the social sciences and includes many government publications.

The Combined Retrospective Index Set to Journals in History, 1838–1974. Washington, D.C.: Carrollton, 1977. Annadel N. Wile, exec. ed.

Periodical Indexes in the Social Sciences and Humanities: A Subject Guide. Metuchen, N.J.: Scarecrow Press, 1978. Lois A Harzfeld.

C. Specialized Periodical Indexes

There are many periodical indexes on specialized topics. If your research takes you into a specialized field, the indexes listed here may be worth looking into.

Agricultural Index; Applied Science and Technology Index; Art Index; Business Periodicals Index; Education Index; Index to Legal Periodicals; Index Medicus; Music Index.

Some specialized periodical indexes of value in historical research are:

Women's Magazines, 1693–1968. London: Michael Joseph, 1970. Cynthia White, comp.

Guide to Current Latin American Periodicals: Humanities and Social Sciences. Gainesville, Fla.: Kallman Publishing, 1961. Irene Zimmerman, ed.

Hispanic American Periodicals Index. Los Angeles: U.C.L.A. Latin American Center Publications, 1974–. Barbara H. Valk, ed.

From Radical Left to Extreme Right. Ann Arbor, Mich.: Campus Publishers, 1970–present. Robert H. Muller et al. This index covers periodicals of dissent and protest.

*American Historical Review: General Index for Volumes XLI–LXX, 1935–1965. New York: Macmillan, 1965.

*Guide to the American Historical Review, 1895–1945. Washington, D.C.: Government Printing Office, 1945. Franklin D. Scott and Elaine Tegler, comps. (This work is found in American Historical Association, *Annual Report for the Year 1944,* Vol. I, pt. 2, pp. 65–292.)

Foreign Affairs 50-Year Index: Vols. 1–50, 1922–1972. New York: Council on Foreign Relations, 1973. Robert J. Palmer, comp.

The Pacific Historical Review: A Cumulative Index to Volumes I–XLIII, 1932–1974. Berkeley: University of California Press, 1976. Anne M. Hager and Everett Gordon, comps.

Fifty Year Index: Mississippi Valley Historical Review, 1914–1964. Bloomington, Ind.: Organization of American Historians, 1973. Francis J. Krauskopf, comp.

Index to Economic Journals. American Economic Association, 1886–present. Homewood, Ill.: R. D. Irwin.

Guide to the Hispanic American Historical Review: 1918–1945, 1945–1955. Durham, N.C.: Duke University Press, 1956–1975. Durham, N.C.: Duke University Press, 1980. Stanley R. Ross, Wilbur Chaffee, eds.

Index to the Canadian Historical Review. Toronto: University of Toronto Press, 1920–.

V. Historical Periodicals

Following is a list of some of the best known historical periodicals published in the United States, Britain, and Canada and written for professional and student researchers. Some of these journals have their own cumulative indexes (like that to the *American Historical Review* listed previously) and thus can be useful places to begin the search for historical material. There are also many highly specialized periodicals in history. For example, most state historical societies publish journals. Be sure to examine periodical indexes that include the journals most closely related to your subject.

A. United States, British, and Canadian Historical Journals

Agricultural History
American Historical Review
American Jewish History
The American Journal of Legal History
American Quarterly
The Americas
Bulletin of the Institute of Historical Research
Business History Review
Cambridge Historical Journal
Canadian Historical Review
Central European History
Current History
Daedalus
Diplomatic History
Economic History Review
Economic Journal
Eighteenth Century Studies
English Historical Review
Ethnohistory
Feminist Studies
Film and History
French Historical Studies
Hispanic American Historical Review
The Historian
Historical Journal
Historical Methods
History
History and Theory
History of Education Quarterly
History of Political Economy
History of Religions
The History Teacher
International Review of Social History
Irish Historical Studies
Isis

Journal of African History
Journal of American History
Journal of Asian Studies
Journal of Black Studies
Journal of British Studies
Journal of Canadian Studies
Journal of Contemporary History
Journal of Ecclesiastical History
Journal of Economic History
Journal of Interdisciplinary History
Journal of Japanese Studies
Journal of Latin American History
Journal of Modern History
Journal of Near Eastern Studies
Journal of Negro History
Journal of Popular Culture
Journal of Religious History
The Journal of Psychohistory
Journal of Social History
Journal of Southern History
Journal of Sports History
Journal of the History of Biology
Journal of the History of Ideas
Journal of Urban History
Labor History
Latin American Research Review
Mid-America
Middle East Review
Oral History Review
Pacific Affairs
Pacific Historical Review
Past and Present
Political Studies
The Public Historian
Renaissance Quarterly
Russian History
Slavic Review
Slavic Studies
Scottish History Review
Social Science History
Speculum

Transactions of the Royal Historical Society
Western Historical Quarterly
William and Mary Quarterly

B. Book Review Indexes

In addition to articles, historical periodicals usually contain reviews of recently published books on historical subjects. (For an example of such a review, see pages 51–52.) If you wish to know the content of a particular book or to find out what other historians thought of it, you can look up the reviews of it. The indexes in the following list organize book reviews by author, title, and sometimes, by subject. They indicate which periodicals reviewed the book and in what issue. If the index is annual, you will need to know the year of publication of the book in which you are interested. Most books are reviewed within one to two years after publication.

Book Review Digest. New York: Wilson, 1905–present. Monthly.
Index to Book Reviews in the Humanities. Detroit: Gale, 1960–present. Annual.
Book Review Digest: Author/Title Index, 1905–1974. New York: Wilson, 1976. Leslie Dunmore-Lieber, ed. 4v.
Cumulative Book Review Citations. New York: Wilson.
*Index to Book Reviews in Historical Periodicals. Metuchen, N.J.: Scarecrow, 1974–.
*Combined Retrospective Index to Book Reviews in Scholarly Journals, 1886–1974. Arlington, Va.: Carrollton Press, 1982, 15v.
New York Times Book Review Index, 1896–1970. New York: New York Times, 1973. 5v.
National Library Service Cumulative Book Review Index, 1905–1974. Princeton: National Library Service Co., 1975. 6v.
Book Review Index. Detroit: Gale, 1965–present. Bimonthly.
Book Review Index: A Master Accumulation, 1969–1979. Detroit: Gale, 1980. Gary C. Tarbert, ed. 7v.

VI. Government Publications and Public Documents

The works included here are guides to books, pamphlets, speeches, treaties, hearings, reports, and so on, published by public agencies. This list, like all others in this appendix, is confined to works in English and is by no means complete. If your research topic is related to governmental affairs at any level, these works can lead you to documents and publications by or about the agencies you are studying. The major publications of the U.S. government are available at many libraries.

A. International Agencies

Guide to League of Nations Publications: A Bibliographical Survey of the Work of the League, 1920–1947. New York: Columbia University Press, 1951. Hans Aufricht, comp.

United Nations Documents Index. New York: United Nations Library, 1950–1977. These volumes are supplemented by *UNDOC: Current Index.*

B. Foreign Government Publications

Manual of Government Publications, United States and Foreign. New York: Appleton-Century-Crofts, 1950. Everett S. Brown, comp.

Great Britain, Parliament: Parliamentary Debates. London: 1803–present.

C. United States Government Publications

*New Guide to Popular Government Publications. Littleton, Colo.: Libraries Unlimited, 1978. Walter L. Newsome, ed.

*Subject Guide to Major United States Government Publications. Chicago: American Library Association, 1968. Ellen P. Jackson, comp.

Monthly Catalogue of United States Government Publications. Washington, D.C.: Government Printing Office, 1895–present.

*Guide to United States Government Publications. McLean, Va.: Documents Index, 1985, John L. Andriot, ed. Cumulative bimonthly supplements.

United States Congressional Committee Hearings Index, 1833–1969. Washington, D.C.: CIS, 1981–.

United States Congressional Committee Prints Index from Earliest Publications through 1969. Washington, D.C.: CIS, 1980. 5v.

United States Serial Set Indexes: American State Papers . . . 1789–1969. Washington, D.C.: CIS, 1975.

Government Publications and Their Use. Washington, D.C.: Brookings Institution, 1969. Laurence Schmeckebier and Roy Eastin, eds.

Subject Guide to Government Reference Books. Littleton, Colo.: Libraries Unlimited, 1972. Sally Wynkoop, ed.

Subject Guide to United States Reference Sources. Littleton, Colo.: Libraries Unlimited, 1985. Judith Schick Robinson, ed.

Government Publications: A Guide to Bibliographic Tools. Washington, D.C.: Library of Congress, 1975. Vladimir M. Palic, comp.

Annotated Bibliography of Bibliographies on Selected Government Publications and Supplementary Guides to the Superintendent of Docu-

ments Classification System. Kalamazoo, Mich.: Western Michigan University, 1967–present. Alexander C. Body, ed.
Cumulative Subject Guide to United States Government Bibliographies, 1924–1973. Arlington, Va.: Carrollton Press, 1976. Edna A. Kanely, comp.
Introduction to United States Public Documents. Littleton, Colo.: Libraries Unlimited, 1983. Joe Morehead.

D. United States State and Local Government Publications

*State Government Reference Publications: An Annotated Bibliography. Littleton, Colo.: Libraries Unlimited, 1981. David W. Parish, ed.
Bibliography of County Histories in Fifty States in 1961. Baltimore: Genealogical Publishing Company, 1963. Clarence Peterson, ed.

For the publications of state historical societies, see Appendix B.

VII. Subject Bibliographies

A subject bibliography lists printed works on a particular topic. The ones listed here are those that the beginning student is likely to be able to obtain. Emphasis has been placed on bibliographies that (1) are written especially for students, (2) are of recent publication or republication and therefore likely to be in new library collections, (3) contain predominantly or solely works in the English language, and (4) are general rather than specialized. Bibliographies that are especially useful to beginning students are designated by an asterisk (*).[2]

A. Disciplines Other Than History

The following bibliographies list works in fields other than history. If an important aspect of your research topic falls under other major branches of knowledge, then you might find valuable materials in nonhistorical publications.

*A Select Bibliography: Asia, Africa, Eastern Europe, Latin America. New York: American University, 1960, plus supplements. These are studies in the social sciences covering the developing countries of the world. For more recent works, see *Cumulative Supplement, 1961–1971* and *1972–1982.*

---

[2]If the title of a bibliography indicates that it is annotated, this means that it not only *lists* books on a particular topic but also provides a brief description of their contents.

Sources of Information in the Social Sciences. Chicago: American Library Association, 1986. William H. Webb, ed.
Sources of Information in the Humanities. Chicago: American Library Association, 1982. 3v. John F. Wilson, ed.
The Humanities: A Selective Guide to Information Sources. Littleton, Colo.: Libraries Unlimited, 1979. A. Robert Rogers, ed.
Social Science Research Handbook. New York: Garland, 1984. Raymond G. McInnis and James W. Scott, eds.

B. Specialized Branches of History

This section contains bibliographies in the history of philosophy, psychology, science, technology, medicine, music, oral history, psychohistory, military history, Jewish history, and family history among others.

Encyclopedia of Medical History. New York: McGraw-Hill, 1985. Roderick E. McGrew, ed.
Dictionary of the History of Ideas. New York: Scribner's, 1968–1974. Philip P. Wiener, ed.
Handbook in the History of Philosophy. New York: Barnes & Noble, 1961.
History of Psychology: A Guide to Information Sources. Detroit: Gale, 1979. Wayne Viney, Michael Wertheimer, and Marilyn Lou Werthheimer, eds.
Bibliography of the History of Technology. Cambridge, Mass.: M.I.T. Press, 1968. Eugene S. Ferguson, ed.
History of Science and Technology: A Select Bibliography for Students. London: Library Association, 1970. K. J. Rider, ed.
History of the Life Sciences: An Annotated Bibliography. New York: Hafner Press, 1974. Pieter Smit, ed.
ISIS Cumulative Bibliography: A Bibliography of the History of Science from Isis Critical Bibliographies 1–90 (1913–1965). London: History of Science Society, 1971–1975. Magda Whitrow, ed. 3v.
Bibliography of the History of Medicine. Bethesda, Md.: National Library of Medicine, 1965–.
New Oxford History of Music. Oxford: Oxford University Press, 1954–1985. 10v.
Bibliography on Oral History. New York: Oral History Association, 1975. Manfred J. Waserman, comp.
Bibliography of Military History: A Revised, Expanded, and Selected Annotated Listing of Reference Sources. West Point, N.Y.: U.S. Military Academy, 1982.

The Encyclopedia of Military History: From 3500 B.C. to the Present.
New York: Harper & Row, 1985. Ernest R. Dupuy and Trevor N.
Dupuy, eds.

The Holocaust: An Annotated Bibliography. Haverford, Pa.: Catholic
Libraries Association, 1985. Harry James Cargas, ed.

The New Standard Jewish Encyclopedia. Garden City, N.Y.: Doubleday,
1977. Geoffrey Wigoder, ed.

Psychohistorical Inquiry: A Comprehensive Research Bibliography.
New York: Garland, 1984. William J. Gilmore, ed.

History of the Family and Kinship: A Select International Bibliography.
Millwood, N.Y.: Kraus International Publications, 1980. Gerald L.
Soliday, ed.

The Family in Past Time: A Guide to the Literature. New York: Garland
Publishing, 1977. James W. Milden.

International Dictionary of Films and Filmmakers. London: St. James
Press, 1990. Nicolas Thomas, ed.

C. General World History

The remainder of this appendix contains the basic source material for
historical research—history bibliographies. Once you have chosen your
research topic, these bibliographies and the reference collection of your
library should be your initial step in finding sources. For the conve-
nience of the beginning student, the list of subject bibliographies is
separated according to the chronological period or geographical area that
the works cover. The bibliographies themselves break down the topics
even further.

Don't expect to find an entire bibliography dedicated to your particular subject. Choose the ones that cover the period or area into which
your own topic falls. Remember, your library will probably not have all
of these books. If the most promising bibliography is not there, try a
different work.

*American Historical Association: A Guide to Historical Literature.
New York: Macmillan, 1961. George F. Howe et al., eds. This work
has chapters on all periods and areas, and on many specialized
topics.

*Historical Abstracts. Santa Barbara, Cal.: ABC-Clio, 1955–present.
Part A: Modern History (1450–1914); Part B: The Twentieth Century (1914–present). Eric H. Boehm, ed. This is the best source for
articles in history journals.

A Select Bibliography of History. Cambridge, Mass.: Henry Adams
   Club, Dept. of History, Harvard University, 1970. D. David Grose,
   ed. This work has chapters on all regions and periods.
Pamphlets. Washington, D.C.: American Historical Association, Service Center for Teachers, 1956–present. These pamphlets contain
   narrative and critical essays on a wide range of topics. Each has a
   bibliography.
Books for College Libraries. Chicago: American Library Association,
   1975. Melvin Voigt and Joseph Treyz, comps. See Volume III: History. It contains chapters on each geographical area.
World Historical Fiction Guide. Metuchen, N.J.: Scarecrow Press,
   1973. Daniel McGarry and Sarah White, eds. If you are studying
   historical novels, this is an important source.
Serial Bibliographies and Abstracts in History: An Annotated Guide.
   Westport, Conn.: Greenwood Press, 1986. David Henige, ed.
Bibliographies in History. Santa Barbara, Cal.: ABC-Clio, 1988.
A Reader's Guide to Contemporary History. Chicago: Quadrangle
   Books, 1972. Bernard Krikler and Walter Laqueur, eds.
Reference Sources in History: An Introductory Guide. Santa Barbara,
   Cal.: ABC-Clio, 1990. Ronald H. Fritze, et al., eds.
World History from Earliest Times to 1800. Oxford: Oxford University
   Press, 1988. H. Judge, ed.
Encyclopedia of Nationalism. New York: Paragon House, 1990. Louis L.
   Snyder, ed.

D. Ancient History

Introduction to Ancient History. Berkeley: University of California,
   1970. Hermann Bengston.
World Guide to Antiquities. New York: Crown, 1975. Seymour Kurtz,
   ed.
The Encyclopedia of Ancient Civilizations. New York: Mayflower Books,
   1980. Arthur Cotterell, ed.
The Cambridge Ancient History. Cambridge: Cambridge University
   Press, 1923–1939, 1951–1954, 1970–1976. This is a multivolume
   historical work with extensive bibliographies.
Illustrated Encyclopedia of the Classical World. New York: Harper &
   Row, 1975. Michael Avi Yonah and Israel Shatzman, eds.
Who Was Who in the Greek World, 776 B.C.–30 B.C. Ithaca, N.Y.:
   Cornell University Press, 1982. Diana Bowder, ed.
Who Was Who in the Roman World, 753 B.C.–A.D. 476. Ithaca, N.Y.:
   Cornell University Press, 1980. Diana Bowder, ed.

The Oxford History of the Classical World. Oxford: Oxford University Press, 1986. John Boardman, et al., eds. An excellent bibliography is included.
The Encyclopedia of Ancient Egypt. New York: Facts on File, 1991. Margaret Bunson, ed.

E. Medieval History

*A Guide to the Study of Medieval History. New York: F. S. Crofts & Sons, 1931. Louis J. Paetow. This guide is updated in a supplement by Gray C. Boyce, Medieval Academy of America, 1980, and by:
*Literature of Medieval History, 1930–1975. Millwood, N.Y.: Kraus International Publisher, 1981. Gray C. Boyce, ed. 5v.
The Illustrated Encyclopedia of Medieval Civilization. New York: Mayflower Books, 1980. Aryeh Grabois, ed.
Medieval European History, 395–1500: A Select Bibliography. London: Historical Association of London, 1963.
Cambridge Medieval History. Cambridge: Cambridge University Press, 1911–1936.
Who's Who in the Middle Ages. New York: Stein and Day, 1980. John Fines, ed.
Dictionary of the Middle Ages. New York: Scribner's, 1982–1989. Joseph R. Strayer, ed.
The Middle Ages: A Concise Encyclopedia. New York: Thames and Hudson/Norton, 1989. H. R. Loyn, ed.
Atlas of Medieval Europe. New York: Facts on File, 1983. Donald Matthew, comp.
Dictionary of Medieval Civilization. New York: Macmillan, 1984. Joseph Dahmus, ed.

F. Early Modern and Modern European History

*Modern European History, 1494–1789: A Select Bibliography. London: Historical Association of London, 1966. Alun Davies, comp.
*Modern European History, 1789–1945: A Select Bibliography. London: Historical Association of London, 1960. William N. Medlicott, comp.
*Cambridge Modern History. Cambridge: Cambridge University Press, 1902–1911; reissued, 1970. These history volumes have large bibliographies. *The New Cambridge Modern History,* however, has no bibliography.
Renaissance Humanism, 1300–1550: A Bibliography of Materials in English. N.Y.: Garland, 1985. Benjamin Kohl, ed.

A Bibliography of Modern History. Cambridge: Cambridge University Press, 1968. John Roach, ed. This bibliography was created to accompany *The New Cambridge Modern History.*

Modern European Imperialism: A Bibliography of Books and Articles, 1815–1972. Boston: G. K. Hall, 1974. John P. Halstead, comp.

Select List of Works on Europe and Europe Overseas, 1715–1815. Oxford: Clarendon Press, 1956. John Bromley and A. Goodwin, eds. Reprinted, Westport, Conn.: Greenwood Press, 1974.

Women in Western European History: A Select Chronological, Geographical and Topical Bibliography from Antiquity to the French Revolution. Westport, Conn.: Greenwood Press, 1982. Linda Frey, Marsha Frey, and Joanne Schneider, eds.

Women in Western European History: A Select Chronological, Geographical, and Topical Bibliography: The Nineteenth and Twentieth Centuries. Westport, Conn.: Greenwood Press, 1984. Linda Frey and Marsha Frey, eds.

The Columbia Dictionary of European Political History Since 1914. Berkeley, Cal.: University of California Press, 1992. John Stevenson, gen. ed.

1. **MODERN EUROPE: FRANCE, ITALY, SPAIN, GERMANY, SCANDINAVIA**

Historical Dictionary of the French Fourth and Fifth Republics, 1946–1991. Westport, Conn.: Greenwood Press, 1992. Wayne Northcutt, ed.

Dictionary of Modern Italian History. Westport, Conn.: Greenwood Press, 1985. Frank J. Coppa, ed.-in-chief.

Modern Italian History: An Annotated Bibliography. Westport, Conn.: Greenwood Press, 1990. Frank J. Cappa and William Roberts, comps. A companion to *Dictionary of Modern Italian History.*

Historical Dictionary of Modern Spain, 1700–1988. Westport, Conn.: Greenwood Press, 1990. Robert W. Kern, ed.-in-chief.

Nazism, Resistance, and the Holocaust in World War II: A Bibliography. Metuchen, N.J.: Scarecrow Press, 1985. Vera Laska, ed.

Dictionary of Scandinavian History. Westport, Conn.: Greenwood Press, 1986. Byron J. Nordstrom, ed.

G. British History

1. **BRITISH HISTORY TO 1789**

A Bibliography of English History to 1485. Oxford: Clarendon Press, 1975. Edgar B. Graves, ed.

Tudor England, 1485–1603: A Bibliographical Handbook. Cambridge: Cambridge University Press, 1968. Mortimer Levine, comp.
A Bibliography of British History, 1603–1714. Oxford: Clarendon Press, 1970. Mary Keeler, ed.
Early Modern British History, 1485–1760. London: Historical Association of London, 1970. Helen Miller and Aubrey Newman, comps.
A Bibliography of British History, 1714–1789. Oxford: Clarendon Press, 1951. Stanley Pargellis and D. J. Medley, eds.

2. BRITISH HISTORY SINCE 1789

British History Since 1760: A Select Bibliography. London: Historical Association of London, 1970. Ian R. Christie, comp.
A Bibliography of British History, 1789–1851. Oxford: Clarendon Press, 1977. Lucy Brown and Ian R. Christie, eds.
A Bibliography of British History, 1851–1914. Oxford: Clarendon Press, 1976. H. J. Hanham, ed.
Modern England, 1901–1970: A Bibliographical Handbook. Cambridge: Cambridge University Press, 1976. Alfred F. Havighurst, comp.
British Economic and Social History: A Bibliographical Guide. Manchester: Manchester University Press, 1976. W. H. Chaloner and R. C. Richardson, eds.
A Dictionary of British History. New York: Stein and Day, 1983. J. P. Kenyon, ed.
The Oxford History of England: Consolidated Index. Oxford: Clarendon/ Oxford University Press, 1991. Richard Raper, comp.
Victorian Britain: An Encyclopedia. New York: Garland, 1988. Sally Mitchell, ed.
The Cambridge Historical Encyclopedia of Great Britain and Ireland. Cambridge: Cambridge University Press, 1985. Christopher Haigh, ed.

3. IRISH, SCOTTISH, AND BRITISH EMPIRE HISTORY

Irish History: A Select Bibliography. London: Historical Association of London, 1972. Edith M. Johnson, comp.
A Dictionary of Irish History Since 1800. Totawa, N.J.: Barnes & Noble, 1980. D. J. Hickey and J. E. Doherty, eds.
A Bibliography of Works Relating to Scotland, 1916–1950. Edinburgh: Edinburgh University Press, 1959–1960. P. D. Hancock, ed.
Cambridge History of the British Empire. Cambridge: Cambridge University Press, 1929–1959. John Rose, Arthur Newton, and Ernest Benians, comps.

A *Chronicle of Irish History Since 1500.* Savage, Md.: Rowman and Littlefield, 1990. J. E. Doherty and D. J. Hickey, eds.

H. East European History

*The Soviet Union and Eastern Europe. New York: Facts on File, 1985. George Schoepflin. This is a general handbook but includes bibliographies.

The American Bibliography of Slavic and East European Studies. Columbus, Ohio: American Association for the Advancement of Slavic Studies, 1957–present.

Junior Slavica: A Selected, Annotated Bibliography of Books in English on Russia and Eastern Europe. Littleton, Colo.: Libraries Unlimited, 1968. Stephan M. Horak, ed.

*The Balkans Since 1453. New York: Rinehart, 1958. Leften S. Stavrianos. There is an extensive bibliography at the end of this work.

Bibliography of American Publications on East Central Europe 1945–1957. Bloomington: Indiana University Press, 1958. Robert F. Byrnes, ed.

Poland's Past and Present: A Select Bibliography of Works in English. Newtonville, Mass.: Oriental Research Partners, 1977. Norman Davies, ed.

Yugoslavia: A Comprehensive English-Language Bibliography. Wilmington, Del.: Scholarly Resources. Francine Friedman, ed.

I. Russian History (and USSR)

The American Bibliography of Slavic and East European Studies. Columbus, Ohio: American Association for the Advancement of Slavic Studies, 1957–present.

*A Bibliography of Works in English on Early Russian History to 1800. New York: Barnes & Noble, 1969. Peter A. Crowther, comp.

*Books in English on the Soviet Union, 1917–1973: A Bibliography. New York: Garland, 1975. David L. Jones, comp.

*A Select Bibliography of Works in English on Russian History, 1801–1917. Oxford: Blackwell, 1962. David Shapiro, ed.

Russia, the USSR, and Eastern Europe: A Bibliographic Guide to English Language Publications, 1964–1974. Littleton, Colo.: Libraries Unlimited, 1978. Stephen M. Horak, ed. Supplements cover: 1975–1980 and 1981–1985.

An Atlas of Russian History. New Haven, Conn.: Yale University Press, 1970. Allen F. Chew, ed.

The Modern Encyclopedia of Russian and Soviet History. Gulf Breeze,
Fla.: Academic International Press, 1976–. Plus supplements.
Russian Economic History. Detroit: Gale, 1977. Daniel R. Kazmer and
Vera Kazmer, eds.
**The Rise and Fall of the Soviet Union: A Selected Bibliography of
Sources in English.* Westport, Conn.: Greenwood Press, 1992.
Abraham J. Edelheit and Hershel Edelheit, eds.
The Soviet Union: A Biographical Dictionary. New York: Macmillan,
1991. Archie Brown, ed.
*Soviet Foreign Policy, 1918–1945: A Guide to Research and Research
Materials.* Wilmington, Del.: Scholarly Resources, 1991. Robert H.
Johnston, ed.
Dictionary of the Russian Revolution. Westport, Conn.: Greenwood
Press, 1989. George Jackson, ed.

J. African History³

Cambridge History of Africa. Cambridge University Press, 1975–
present. 8v.
*Africa South of the Sahara: A Bibliography for Undergraduate Librar-
ies.* Williamsport, Pa.: Bro-Dart, 1971. Peter Duignan, ed.
*Africa and the World: An Introduction to the History of Sub-Saharan
Africa from Antiquity to 1840.* San Francisco: Chandler, 1972. Pe-
ter Duignan and Lewis H. Gann, eds.
The African Experience. Evanston, Ill.: Northwestern University Press,
1970. John N. Paden and Edward W. Soja, eds.
*An Atlas of African History. New York: Africana Publisher, 1978. J. D.
Fage, ed.
Historical Dictionary of ———. Metuchen, N.J.: Scarecrow Press,
1972–. This is a series of historical dictionaries including separate
volumes for most African nations.
African Newspapers in Selected American Libraries. Washington, D.C.:
Library of Congress, 1965.
*A Select Bibliography on Traditional and Modern Africa. Syracuse,
N.Y.: Syracuse University Press, 1968. Peter Gutkind and John B.
Webster, eds.
Makers of Modern Africa. London: Africa Journal Ltd., 1981.
South African History: A Bibliographic Guide with Special Reference to

---

³For the northern African states that border on the Mediterranean, see Near and Middle
Eastern History.

Territorial Expansion and Colonization. New York: Garland Publishing, 1984. Naomi Musiker, ed.

Dictionary of African Historical Biography. University of California Press, 1986. Mark R. Lipschultz and R. Kent Rasmusson, eds.

K. Near and Middle Eastern History

*The Near and Middle East: An Introduction to History and Bibliography. Washington, D.C.: American Historical Association, 1959. Roderic H. Davison, ed.

Concise Encyclopedia of the Middle East. Washington, D.C.: Public Affairs Press, 1973. Mehdi Heravi, ed.

*The Islamic Near East and North Africa: An Annotated Guide to Books in English for Non-Specialists. Littleton, Colo.: Libraries Unlimited, 1977. David W. Littlefield, ed.

Middle East and Islam: A Bibliographical Introduction. Geneva: Inter Documentation, 1979. Derek Hopwood and Diana Grimwood-Jones, eds.

The Arab-Israeli Conflict: A Historical, Political, Social and Military Bibliography. Santa Barbara, Cal.: ABC-Clio, 1976. Ronald M. Devore, ed.

*Concise Encyclopedia of Arabic Civilizations. New York: Praeger, 1960–1966. Stephan and Nandy Ronart, eds.

Atlas of Islamic History. Princeton, N.J.: Princeton University Press, 1954. Harry W. Hazard, ed.

*Books on Asia from the Near East to the Far East: A Guide for General Readers. Toronto: University of Toronto Press, 1981. Eleazir Birnbaum, ed.

Encyclopedia of Islam. Leiden, Netherlands: E. J. Brill, 1960–present. C.E. Botsworth, et al., eds.

The Cambridge Encyclopedia of the Middle East and North Africa. Cambridge: Cambridge University Press, 1988. Trevor Mostyn, exec. ed.

The Oxford Dictionary of Byzantium. Oxford: Oxford University Press, 1991. Alexander P. Kazhdan, ed.

L. General Asian History

Cumulative Bibliography of Asian Studies, 1941–1965, 1966–1970. Boston: G. K. Hall, 1972.

*Books on Asia from the Near East to the Far East: A Guide for General Readers. Toronto: University of Toronto Press, 1971. Eleazir Birnbaum, ed.

Oriental and Asian Bibliography. Hamden, Conn.: Archon, 1966. J. D. Pearson, ed.

*Asia: A Selected and Annotated Guide to Reference Works. Cambridge, Mass.: M.I.T. Press, 1971. G. Raymond Nunn, ed.

Bibliography of Asian Studies. Ann Arbor, Mich.: Association for Asian Studies, 1941–present.

Historical and Cultural Dictionary of ———. Metuchen, N.J.: Scarecrow Press, 1972–present. This is a series of dictionaries including separate volumes for most Asian nations.

*Encyclopedia of Asian History. New York: Scribner's, 1988. Ainslis T. Embree, ed.

1. INDIAN, PAKISTANI, AND SRI LANKAN HISTORY

*India: A Critical Bibliography. Tucson: University of Arizona Press, 1980. J. Michael Mahar, ed.

A Dictionary of Indian History. New York: Braziller, 1967. Sachchidananda Bhattacharya.

*The History of India: Its Study and Interpretation. Washington, D.C.: American Historical Association, 1965. R. D. Crane.

Introduction to the Civilization of India: Handbook. Chicago: University of Chicago Press, 1961.

*Cambridge History of India. New York: Macmillan, 1922–1953. See bibliography at end of volumes.

*An Historical Atlas of South Asia. Chicago: University of Chicago Press, 1978. Joseph E. Schwartzberg, ed.

2. SOUTHEAST ASIAN HISTORY

*Southeast Asia: A Critical Bibliography. Tucson: University of Arizona Press, 1969. Kennedy G. Tregonning, ed.

*Southeast Asian History: A Bibliographic Guide. New York: Praeger, 1962. Stephen Hay and Margaret Case, eds.

Southeast Asia: An Annotated Bibliography. Westport, Conn.: Greenwood Press, 1968. Cecil C. Hobbs, ed.

Vietnam: A Comprehensive Bibliography. Metuchen, N.J.: Scarecrow Press, 1973. John H. M. Chen, ed.

Vietnam: A Guide to Reference Sources. Boston: G. K. Hall, 1977. Michael Cotter, ed.

The Wars in Vietnam, Cambodia, and Laos, 1945–1982: A Bibliographic Guide. Santa Barbara, Cal.: ABC-Clio, 1984. Richard Dean Burns and Milton Leitenberg, eds.

3. CHINESE HISTORY

China: A Critical Bibliography. Tucson: University of Arizona Press, 1962. Charles O. Hucker, ed.

Chinese History: A Bibliographical Review. Washington, D.C.: American Historical Association, 1958. Charles O. Hucker, ed.

Historical Atlas of China. Chicago: Aldine, 1966. Albert Herrmann, ed.

China and America: A Bibliography of Interactions, Foreign and Domestic. Honolulu: University of Hawaii Press, 1972. James M. McCutcheon, comp.

*Dictionary of Chinese History. London: Frank Cass, 1979. Michael Dillon, ed.

Chinese History: A Bibliography. New York: Gordon Press, 1978. Leona Rasmussen Phillips, ed.

4. JAPANESE AND KOREAN HISTORY

*Japanese History: New Dimensions of Approach and Understanding. Washington, D.C.: American Historical Association, 1966. John W. Hall, ed.

A Guide to Reference and Research Materials on Korean History: An Annotated Bibliography. Honolulu: East-West Center, 1968. William E. Hentworth, ed.

Dictionary of Japanese History. New York: Walker, 1968. Joseph M. Goedertier.

*Japan and Korea: A Critical Bibliography. Westport, Conn.: Greenwood Press, 1982. Bernard Silberman, ed.

The Cambridge Dictionary of Japan, Volume 4: Early Modern Japan. Cambridge: Cambridge University Press, 1991. John Whitney Hall, ed.

Japanese History and Culture from Ancient to Modern Times: Seven Basic Bibliographies. New York: Markus Wiener, 1993. John Dower and Timothy George, eds.

M. Latin American and Caribbean History

Handbook of Latin American Studies. Cambridge, Mass.: Harvard University Press, 1936–1947; and Gainesville: University of Florida Press, 1948–present. Annual volume.

*Latin America: A Guide to the Historical Literature. Austin: University of Texas Press, 1971. Charles C. Griffin, ed.

A Guide to Latin American Studies. Los Angeles: University of California, 1967. Martin H. Sable, ed.

Latin America and the Caribbean: A Bibliographic Guide to Works in English. Coral Gables: University of Miami Press, 1967. Stojan A. Bayitch, ed.

Who's Who in Latin America. Stanford: Stanford University Press, 1951. Reprinted by Blaine Ethridge Books, Detroit, 1971. Ronald Hilton, ed.

A Bibliography of Latin American Bibliographies Published in Periodicals. Metuchen, N.J.: Scarecrow Press, 1976. Arthur E. Gropp, ed. 2v.

The Complete Caribbeana, 1900–1975: A Bibliographical Guide to the Scholarly Literature. Millwood, N.Y.: KTO Press, 1978. Comitas Lambros, ed.

The Cambridge Encyclopedia of Latin America and the Caribbean. Cambridge: Cambridge University Press, 1992. Simon Collier et al., eds.

*A Guide to the History of Brazil, 1500–1822: The Literature in English. Santa Barbara, Cal.: ABC-Clio, 1980. Francis A. Dutra, ed.

Index to Latin American Periodical Literature, 1929–1960. New York: G. K. Hall, 1962. Pan American Union. Updated through 1970 by G. K. Hall, 1980.

*Latin America, Spain and Portugal: A Selected and Annotated Bibliographical Guide to Books Published in the United States, 1954–1974. Metuchen, N.J.: Scarecrow Press, 1977. A. C. Wilgus, ed. and comp.

Latin America: A Guide to Economic History, 1830–1930. Berkeley: University of California Press, 1977. Stanley Stein and R. Cortés Conde, eds.

Encyclopedia of Latin America. New York: McGraw-Hill, 1974. Helen Delpar, ed.

Historical Dictionary of ———. Metuchen, N.J.: Scarecrow Press. This is a series of historical dictionaries including separate volumes for most Latin American nations.

Latin American Politics: A Historical Bibliography. Santa Barbara, Cal.: ABC-Clio, 1986.

N. Canadian History

Encyclopedia Canadiana. Toronto: Grolier, 1977.

Bibliographia Canadiana. Don Mills, Ont.: Longman Canada Limited, 1973. Claude Thibault, comp.

The Oxford Companion to Canadian History and Literature. Toronto:

Oxford University Press, 1967, *Supplement,* 1973. Norah Story, comp.

Canadian Reference Sources: A Select Guide. Ottawa: Canadian Library Association, 1973, *Supplement,* 1975. Dorothy E. Ryder, ed.

*Canada Since 1867: A Bibliographical Guide. Toronto: Samuel Stevens, 1977. J. L. Granatstein and Paul Stevens, eds.

Western Canada Since 1870: A Select Bibliography and Guide. Vancouver: University of British Columbia Press, 1978. Alan F. J. Artibise, ed.

Bibliography of Ontario History, 1867–1976: Cultural, Economic, Political and Social. Buffalo: University of Toronto Press, 1980. Olga B. Bishop, ed. 2v.

Economic History of Canada: A Guide for Information Sources. Detroit: Gale, 1978. Trevor J. O. Dick, ed.

Canadian Political Parties, 1867–1968: A Historical Bibliography. Toronto: Macmillan, 1977. Grace F. Heggie, ed.

Canadian Urban History: A Select Bibliography. Sudbury: Laurentian University Press, 1972. Gilbert A. Stelter, ed.

An Historical Atlas of Canada. Don Mills, Ont.: Nelson, 1975. Donald G. G. Kerr, ed.

Historical Atlas of Canada. Toronto: University of Toronto Press, 1987. R. Cole Harris and Donald Kerr, eds.

The Canadian Encyclopedia. Edmonton: Hurtig, 1985. James H. March, ed.-in-chief.

O. United States History

In the case of United States history, the bibliographies have been broken down in terms of certain topics of special interest to students.

Many of this first group of bibliographies have separate chapters on specialized topics.

*Harvard Guide to American History. Cambridge, Mass.: Harvard University Press, 1974. Oscar Handlin et al., eds. Chapters six through thirty contain detailed reading lists for many periods and topics in United States history. Revised, 1979.

*The Reader's Companion to American History. Boston, Mass.: Houghton Mifflin, 1991. Eric Foner and John A. Garraty, eds.

*Writings on American History. Washington, D.C.: American Historical Association, 1956; and Millwood, N.Y.: KTO Press, 1976–present. The original series of volumes covers (with two brief lapses) books and articles written between 1902 and 1961. The new series is now

annual and covers only articles written since 1962. Coverage of books is continued in:

Writings on American History, 1962–1973: A Subject Bibliography of Books and Monographs. White Plains, N.Y.: Kraus International Publications, 1985. James R. Masterson, comp. 10v.

Writings on American History, 1962–1973: A Subject Bibliography of Articles. Millwood, N.Y.: KTO Press, 1976. James J. Dougherty, ed. 4v. This work is continued in:

Writings on American History: A Subject Bibliography of Articles. 1974–1990.

America: History and Life. Santa Barbara, Cal.: ABC-Clio, 1954– present. After 1965, titled *America: History and Life: A Guide to Periodical Literature.* Each volume now has four parts: (1) abstracts of journal articles, (2) an index to book reviews, (3) a bibliography of articles and dissertations, and (4) an annual index. The best source for articles on United States history.

Handbook for Research in American History: A Guide to Bibliographies and Other Reference Works. Lincoln: University of Nebraska Press, 1987. Francis Paul Prucha, ed.

A Bibliography of American Autobiographies. Madison: University of Wisconsin Press, 1961. Louis Kaplan et al., comps. An important source if you are researching the life of a historical figure.

Dictionary of American History. New York: Scribner's, 1942–1961. James T. Adams and Roy V. Coleman, eds. Revised, 1976.

Concise Dictionary of American History. New York: Scribner's, 1983. David W. Voorhees, ed. This is an abridgement of the eight-volume *Dictionary of American History.*

Encyclopedia of American Political History: Studies of the Principal Movements and Ideas. New York: Scribner's, 1984. Jack P. Greene, ed. 3v.

U.S.-iana, 1650–1950: A Selective Bibliography. New York: Bowker, 1978. Wright Howes, ed.

Recently Published Articles. Washington, D.C.: American Historical Association, 1976–1990.

The Encyclopedia of Colonial and Revolutionary America. N.Y.: Facts on File, 1989. John Faragher, ed.

History of the United States of America: A Guide to Information Sources. Detroit: Gale, 1977. Ernest Cassara, ed.

Encyclopedia of American History. New York: Harper & Row, 1982. Richard B. Morris, ed.

The American Heritage Pictorial Atlas of United States History. New
York: American Heritage Publishing Co., 1966.
A Guide to the Study of the United States of America. Washington,
D.C.: Library of Congress, 1960. *Supplement,* 1976. This work
covers all fields of knowledge. It has several chapters on aspects of
United States history.

For sources on the United States government, see "United States Government Publications" on pages 126–127.

1. REGIONAL, STATE, COUNTY, AND LOCAL UNITED STATES HISTORY

The sources listed here can be supplemented by the appropriate sections of the *Harvard Guide to American History, Writings on American
History,* and *America: History and Life.*

*A Classified Bibliography of the Periodical Literature of the Trans-
Mississippi West, 1811–1967.* Westport, Conn.: Greenwood Press,
1972. Oscar O. Winther, ed.
Directory of State and Local History Periodicals. Chicago: American
Library Association, 1977. Milton Crouch and Hans Raum, comps.
A Bibliography of American County Histories. Baltimore: Genealogical
Publishing Co., 1985. P. William Filby.
*State Censuses: An Annotated Bibliography to Censuses of Population
Taken after 1790 by States and Territories of the United States.* New
York: Burt Franklin, 1969. Henry J. Dubester, ed.
The Encyclopedia of Southern History. Baton Rouge: Louisiana State
University, 1979. David C. Roller, ed.
The Frontier and the American West. Northbrook, Ill.: AHM Publish-
ing, 1976. Rodman W. Paul and Richard W. Etulain, comps.
The Old South. Northbrook, Ill.: AHM Publishing, 1980. Fletcher M.
Greene and J. Isaac Copeland, comps.
The New South. Northbrook, Ill.: AHM Publishing, forthcoming. Paul
M. Gaston, comp.
**Directory of Historical Organizations in the United States and Canada,
1990.* Nashville: American Association for State and Local History,
1990. Mary Bray Wheeler, comp. This volume includes the ad-
dresses of state and local historical societies.
Encyclopedia of Southern Culture. Chapel Hill, N.C.: University of
North Carolina Press, 1989. Charles Reagan Wilson and William
Ferris, eds.
Localized History Series. New York: Teachers College Press, 1965–
present. Clifford L. Lord, ed. A multivolume series; each volume

contains a bibliography of works on a separate state, region, city, or ethnic group.

United States Local Histories in the Library of Congress: A Bibliography. Baltimore: Magna Carta, 1975. Marion J. Kaminkow, ed.

Consolidated Bibliography of County Histories in Fifty States in 1961. Baltimore: Genealogical Publishing Co., 1963. Clarence Peterson, ed.

2. SPECIFIC PERIODS

Though now somewhat out of date, the best bibliographies for the study of specific periods of United States history are the Goldentree Series published by Harlan Davidson, Inc., Arlington Heights, Illinois. The relevant items in this series, in chronological order, are listed below.

The American Colonies in the Seventeenth Century (1971). Alden T. Vaughan, comp.

The American Colonies in the Eighteenth Century, 1689–1763 (1969). Jack P. Greene, comp.

The American Revolution (1973). John Shy, comp.

Confederation, Constitution and Early National Period, 1781–1815 (1975). E. James Ferguson, comp.

The Era of Good Feeling and the Age of Jackson, 1816–1841 (1979). Edwin A. Miles and Robert Remini, comps.

Manifest Destiny and the Coming of the Civil War, 1841–1860 (1970). Don E. Fehrenbacher, comp.

The Nation in Crisis, 1861–1877 (1969). David Donald, comp.

The Gilded Age, 1877–1896 (1973). Vincent P. DeSantis, comp.

The Progressive Era and the Great War, 1896–1920 (1978). Arthur S. Link and W. M. Leary, Jr., comps.

The New Era and the New Deal, 1920–1940 (1981). Robert E. Burke and Richard Lowitt, comps.

The Second World War and the Atomic Age, 1940–1973 (1975). E. David Cronon and Theodore B. Rosenof, comps.

3. DIPLOMATIC HISTORY

Guide to the Diplomatic History of the United States, 1775–1921. Washington, D.C.: Government Printing Office, 1935. Samuel F. Bemis and Grace G. Griffin, eds. Reprinted, 1959.

*Foreign Affairs Bibliography: A Selected and Annotated List of Books on International Relations [1919–present]. New York: Harper & Row, 1933, 1943, 1953; and R. R. Bowker, 1964. Vol. 1 covers 1919–

1932; Vol. II, 1932–1942; Vol. III, 1942–1952; Vol. IV, 1952–1962; Vol. V, 1962–1972.

Foreign Relations of the United States. Washington, D.C.: Government Printing Office, 1861–present. United States Department of State. These volumes are issued annually and contain actual diplomatic correspondence. These are *primary* sources rather than bibliographies. They are listed because many libraries have them.

A Bibliography of United States–Latin American Relations Since 1810. Lincoln: University of Nebraska Press, 1968. David F. Trask et al., eds. *Supplement,* 1979.

American Diplomatic History Before 1900. Northbrook, Ill.: AHM Publishing, 1978. Norman A. Graebner.

American Diplomatic History Since 1890. Northbrook, Ill.: AHM Publishing, 1975. Wilton B. Fowler, comp.

Dictionary of American Diplomatic History. Westport, Conn.: Greenwood Press, 1989. John E. Findling, ed.

Encyclopedia of American Foreign Policy: Studies of the Principal Movements and Ideas. New York: Scribner's, 1978. Alex DeConde, ed. 3v.

United States Foreign Relations. Detroit: Gale Press, 1980. Elmer Plischke, ed.

Guide to American Foreign Relations Since 1700. Santa Barbara, Cal.: ABC-Clio, 1983. Richard Dean Burns, ed.

Origins, Evolution and Nature of the Cold War: An Annotated Bibliography. Santa Barbara, Cal.: ABC-Clio, 1985. J. L. Black, ed.

Writing About Vietnam: A Bibliography of the Literature of the Vietnam Conflict. Boston, Mass.: G. K. Hall, 1989. Sandra M. Wittman, ed.

4. LABOR HISTORY

American Working Class History: A Representative Bibliography. New York: R. R. Bowker, 1983. Maurice Neufeld, Daniel J. Leab, and Dorothy Swanson.

Biographical Dictionary of American Labor, rev. ed. Westport, Conn.: Greenwood Press, 1984. Gary Fink, ed.

Labor Unions. Westport, Conn.: Greenwood Press, 1977. Gary M. Fink, ed. Contains a brief history and bibliography for each major union.

American Labor History and Comparative Labor Movements. Tucson: University of Arizona Press, 1973. James C. McBrearty, comp.

Labor in America: A Historical Bibliography. Santa Barbara, Cal.: ABC-Clio, 1985.

5. BUSINESS AND ECONOMIC HISTORY

The Economic History of the United States Prior to 1860: An Annotated Bibliography. Santa Barbara, Cal.: ABC-Clio, 1976. Thomas Orsagh et al., eds.

American Economic History Before 1860. Northbrook, Ill.: AHM Publishing, 1969. George R. Taylor, comp.

American Economic History Since 1860. Northbrook, Ill.: AHM Publishing, 1971. Edward C. Kirkland, comp.

American Economic and Business History: A Guide to Information Sources. Detroit: Gale, 1971. Robert W. Lovett, ed.

Biographical Dictionary of American Business Leaders. Westport, Conn.: Greenwood Press, 1983. John Ingham, ed. 4v.

American Economic History: A Guide to Information Sources. Detroit: Gale, 1980. William K. Hutchinson, ed.

Encyclopedia of American Economic History. New York: Scribner's, 1980. Glenn Porter, ed. 3v.

Dictionary of United States Economic History. Westport, Conn. Greenwood Press, 1992. James S. Olson, ed.

6. AFRICAN-AMERICAN HISTORY

A Layman's Guide to Negro History. New York: McGraw-Hill, 1967. Erwin A. Salk, ed.

The Negro in America: A Bibliography. Cambridge, Mass.: Harvard University Press, 1970. Elizabeth W. Miller, comp.

A Bibliographic History of Blacks in America Since 1528. New York: McKay, 1971. Edgar A. Toppin, ed.

Blacks in America: Bibliographical Essays. Garden City, N.Y.: Doubleday, 1971. James M. McPherson et al.

Black History Viewpoints: A Selected Bibliographical Guide to Resources for Afro-American and African History. Westport, Conn.: African Bibliographic Center, 1969.

Black Studies: A Bibliography for the Use of Schools, Libraries and the General Reader. Brooklawn, N.J.: McKinley, 1973. Leonard B. Irwin, comp.

The Black Family in the United States: A Selected Bibliography of Annotated Books, Articles, and Dissertations on Black Families in

America. Westport, Conn.: Greenwood Press, 1978. Lenwood G. Davis, ed.
Encyclopedia of Black America. New York: McGraw-Hill, 1981. Augustus Low, ed.
Afro-American History: A Bibliography. Santa Barbara: ABC-Clio, 1981. Dwight L. Smith, ed.
The Black American Reference Book. Englewood Cliffs, N.J.: Prentice-Hall, 1976. Mabel M. Smythe, ed.
Dictionary of American Negro Biography. New York: W. W. Norton, 1982. Rayford W. Logan and Michael Winston, eds.

7. MEXICAN-AMERICAN HISTORY

Mexican-American History: A Critical Selective Bibliography. Santa Barbara, Cal.: Mexican-American Historical Society, 1969.
*The Mexican American: A Selected and Annotated Bibliography. Stanford, Cal.: Stanford University Press, 1971. Luis G. Nogales, ed.
Bibliografía de Aztlán: An Annotated Chicano Bibliography. San Diego, Cal.: San Diego State College, 1971. Ernie Barrios, comp.
*A Bibliography for Chicano History. Westport, Conn.: Greenwood Press, 1984. Matt S. Meier and Feliciano Rivera, comps.
Reference Materials on Mexican Americans: An Annotated Bibliography. Metuchen, N.J.: Scarecrow Press, 1976. Richard P. Woods, ed.
*Bibliography of Mexican-American History. Westport, Conn.: Greenwood Press, 1984. Matt S. Meier, comp.
Dictionary of Mexican American History. Westport, Conn.: Greenwood Press, 1981. Matt Meier and Feliciano Rivera, eds.

8. PUERTO RICAN HISTORY

*Puerto Ricans on the United States Mainland. Totowa, N.J.: Rowman and Littlefield, 1972. Francesco Cordasco, ed.
*The Puerto Ricans: An Annotated Bibliography. New York: Bowker, 1973. Paquita Vivó, ed.
*An Annotated, Selected Puerto Rican Bibliography. New York: Columbia University Press, 1972. Enrique R. Bravo, comp.
The Puerto Ricans 1493–1973: A Chronology and Fact Book. Dobbs Ferry, N.Y.: Oceana, 1973. Francesco Cordasco, ed.
Puerto Ricans and Other Minority Groups in the Continental United States: An Annotated Bibliography. Detroit: Blaine Ethridge Books, 1979.
Historical Dictionary of Puerto Rico and the United States Virgin Islands. Metuchen, N.J.: Scarecrow Press, 1973. Kenneth Farr, comp.

9. WOMEN'S HISTORY

The American Woman in Colonial and Revolutionary Times, 1565–1800: A Syllabus with Bibliography. Westport, Conn.: Greenwood Press, 1975. Eugenie Leonard et al.

Women's Magazines, 1693–1968. London: Michael Joseph, 1970. Cynthia White, comp.

Notable American Women, 1607–1950: A Biographical Dictionary. Cambridge, Mass.: Harvard University Press, 1971. Edward T. James, ed. 3v. Supplemented by *Notable American Women: The Modern Period.* 1980. This volume includes women who died from 1951 through 1975.

The Female Experience in Eighteenth- and Nineteenth-Century America: A Guide to the History of American Women. New York: Garland, 1982. Jill Conway, ed.

The Female Experience in Twentieth-Century America: A Guide to the History of American Women. New York: Garland, 1986. Jill Conway, ed.

Women in American History: A Bibliography. Santa Barbara, Cal.: ABC-Clio, 1979. Cynthia E. Harrison, ed.

Research Guide in Women's Studies. Morristown, N.J.: General Learning Press, 1974. Naomi B. Lynn, Ann B. Matasar, and Marie Rosenberg, eds.

Women's Studies Encyclopedia: History, Philosophy, and Religion. Vol. III. Westport, Conn.: Greenwood Press, 1991. Helen Tierney, ed.

Handbook of American Women's History. New York: Garland, 1990. Angela Howard Zophy, ed.

10. GENERAL IMMIGRANT AND ETHNIC HISTORY

General immigrant and ethnic history bibliographies are the best to use if you are researching the history of a minority group not listed separately in this appendix or if you are unsure which group you wish to study.

Minority Studies: A Select Annotated Bibliography. Boston: G. K. Hall, 1975. Priscilla Oaks, ed.

A Handbook of American Minorities. New York: New York University Press, 1976. Wayne C. Miller.

A Comprehensive Bibliography for the Study of American Minorities. New York: New York University Press, 1976. Wayne C. Miller. 2v.

Brief Ethnic Bibliography: An Annotated Guide to the Ethnic Experience in the United States. Cambridge, Eng.: Langdon Associates, 1976. Joseph J. Barton, comp.

Encyclopedic Dictionary of Ethnic Newspapers and Periodicals in the United States. Littleton, Colo.: Libraries Unlimited, 1972. Lubomyr S. Wynar, ed.

*Harvard Encyclopedia of American Ethnic Groups. Cambridge: Harvard University Press, 1980. Stephen Thernstrom, ed.

Immigration and Ethnicity: A Guide to Information Sources. Detroit: Gale, 1977. John D. Buenker and Nicholas C. Burckel, eds.

Dictionary of American Immigrant History. Metuchen, N.J.: Scarecrow Press, 1990. Francesco Cordasco, ed.

11. EUROPEAN IMMIGRANT AND ETHNIC HISTORY

*European Immigration and Ethnicity in the United States and Canada: A Bibliography. Santa Barbara, Cal.: ABC-Clio, 1983. David L. Brye, ed.

A Bibliographic Guide to Greeks in the United States, 1890–1968. New York: Center for Migration Studies, 1970. Michael N. Cutsumbis, ed.

German American History and Life: A Guide to Information Sources. Detroit: Gale Research Company, 1980. Michael Kereztesi and Gary Cocozzoli, eds.

Hungarians in the United States and Canada: A Bibliography. Minneapolis: Immigration History Research Center, 1977. Joseph Szeplaki, ed.

The British in America 1578–1970: A Chronology and Fact Book. Dobbs Ferry, N.Y.: Oceana, 1972. Howard B. Furer, ed. Volume covers the English, Scotch, Welsh, and Scotch-Irish.

The ——— in America: A Chronology and Fact Book. Dobbs Ferry, N.Y.: Oceana, 1971–present. This is a series with separate volumes on the Germans, Scandinavians, Italians, Poles, Dutch, Jews, Hungarians, and others.

Italian Americans: A Guide to Information Sources. Detroit: Gale, 1978. Francesco Cordasco, ed.

12. ASIAN IMMIGRANT AND ETHNIC HISTORY

*Asian American Studies: An Annotated Bibliography and Research Guide. Westport, Conn.: Greenwood Press, 1989. Hyung-Chan Kim, ed.

Asian Americans: An Annotated Bibliography for Public Libraries. Chicago: Amerian Library Association, 1977.

Asians in America: A Selected, Annotated Bibliography. University of California Press, 1983. Isao Fujimoto, ed.

China and America: A Bibliography of Interactions, Foreign and Domestic. Honolulu: University of Hawaii Press, 1972. James M. McCutcheon, comp.

Dictionary of Asian American History. Westport, Conn.: Greenwood Press, 1986. Hyung-Chan Kim, ed.

13. NATIVE AMERICAN HISTORY

Handbook of American Indians North of Mexico. New York: Rowman and Littlefield, 1979. Frederick W. Hodge et al. This is a reprint of a 1910 work.

Reference Encyclopedia of the American Indian. Rye, N.Y.: Todd, 1978. Bernard Klein and Daniel Icolari, eds.

Encyclopedia of Native American Tribes. New York: Facts on File, 1988. Carl Waldman, ed.

Indians of North America: Methods and Sources for Library Research. Hamden, Conn.: Library Professional Pubs., 1983. Marilyn L. Haas, ed.

Indians of the United States and Canada: A Bibliography. Santa Barbara, Cal.: ABC-Clio, 1974. Dwight L. Smith, ed.

Native American Periodicals and Newspapers, 1828–1982: Bibliography, Publishing Record, and Holdings. Westport, Conn.: Greenwood Press, 1984. Maureen Hardy, comp.

Ethnographic Bibliography of North America. New Haven, Conn.: HRAF Press, 1975. George P. Murdock and Timothy J. O'Leary, eds. 5v.

A Concise Dictionary of Indian Tribes of North America. Algonac, Mich.: Reference Publishers, 1979.

Handbook of North American Indians. Washington, D.C.: Smithsonian Institution, 1978–present. William C. Sturtevant, gen. ed. Published yearly. Twenty volumes projected.

A Bibliographical Guide to the History of Indian-White Relations in the United States. University of Chicago Press, 1977. Francis Paul Prucha, ed. Continued in:

Indian-White Relations in the United States: A Bibliography of Works Published 1975–1980. Lincoln: University of Nebraska Press, 1982. Francis Paul Prucha, ed.

Guide to Research on North American Indians. American Library Association, 1983. Arlene B. Hirschfelder et al., eds.

14. SOCIAL, CULTURAL, AND RELIGIOUS HISTORY

Social History of the United States: A Guide to Information Sources.
Detroit: Gale, 1979. D. Tingley, ed.
American Social History Before 1860. Northbrook, Ill.: AHM Publishing, 1970. Gerald N. Grob, comp.
American Social History Since 1860. Northbrook, Ill.: AHM Publishing, 1970. Robert H. Bremner, comp.
Encyclopedia of American Social History. New York: Scribner's, 1993. Mary K. Cayton, Elliott J. Gorn, Peter W. Williams, eds.
A Dictionary of American Social Change. Malabar, Fla.: Kreiger Publishing Company, 1982. Louis Filler.
Social Reform and Reaction in America: An Annotated Bibliography. Santa Barbara, Cal.: ABC-Clio, 1984.
Urban America: A Historical Bibliography. Santa Barbara, Cal.: ABC-Clio, 1983. Neil L. Shumsky and Timothy Crimmins, eds.
Urban History. Detroit: Gale Press, 1981. John D. Buenker, ed.
United States Cultural History: A Guide to Information Sources. Detroit: Gale, 1980. Philip I. Mitterling.
A Critical Bibliography of Religion in America. Princeton, N.J.: Princeton University Press, 1961. Nelson R. Burr, ed.
Religion in American Life. Northbrook, Ill.: AHM Publishing, 1971. Nelson R. Burr, comp.
Historical Atlas of Religion in America. New York: Harper & Row, 1976. Edwin S. Gaustad.
Encyclopedia of the American Religious Experience. New York: Scribner's, 1988.

15. CONSTITUTIONAL, LEGAL, AND MILITARY HISTORY

A Selected Bibliography of American Constitutional History. Santa Barbara, Cal.: ABC-Clio, 1975. Stephen M. Millett.
American Constitutional Development. Northbrook, Ill.: AHM Publishing, 1977. Alpheus T. Mason, comp.
The Literature of American Legal History. New York: Oceana Pubs., 1985. William E. Nelson and John P. Reid.
Encyclopedia of the American Judicial System. New York: Scribner's, 1987. Robert J. Janosik, ed.
Encyclopedia of the American Constitution. New York: Macmillan, 1986. Supplement, 1992. Leonard Levy, ed.-in-chief.
Reference Guide to United States Military History, 1607–1815. New York: Facts on File, 1991. Charles R. Shrader, ed.

The Blackwell Encyclopedia of the American Revolution. Cambridge, Mass.: Basil Blackwell, 1991. Jack P. Greene and J. R. Pole, eds.

Dictionary of the Vietnam War. Westport, Conn.: Greenwood Press, 1988. James S. Olson, ed.

Guide to the Sources of United States Military History. Hamden, Conn.: Archon Books, 1975. Robin Higham. A supplement was published in 1981.

Civil War Books: A Critical Bibliography. Baton Rouge: Louisiana State University Press, 1968. Allan Nevins, ed.

Bibliographic Guide to the Two World Wars. New York: Bowker, 1977. Gywn M. Bayliss, ed.

16. POLITICAL HISTORY

Political Parties and Elections in the United States: An Encyclopedia. New York: Garland, 1991. L. Sandy Maisel, gen. ed. 2 vols.

Guide to the Presidency. Washington, D.C.: Congressional Quarterly, 1989. Michael Nelson, ed.

Guide to United States Elections. Washington, D.C.: Congressional Quarterly, 1985. John L. Moore, ed.

United States Politics and Elections. Detroit: Gale Press, 1978. David J. Maurer, ed.

The American Presidency: A Historical Bibliography. Santa Barbara, Cal.: ABC-Clio, 1984.

Herbert Hoover: A Bibliography of His Times and Presidency. Wilmington, Del.: Scholarly Resources, 1991. Richard D. Burns, comp.

Dwight D. Eisenhower: A Bibliography of His Times and Presidency. Wilmington, Del.: Scholarly Resources, 1991. R. Alton Lee, comp.

Encyclopedia of the American Left. Urbana, Ill.: University of Illinois Press, 1992. Mari Jo Buhle, ed.

Historical Dictionary of the Progressive Era, 1890–1920. Westport, Conn.: Greenwood Press, 1988. John D. Buenker, ed.

17. MISCELLANEOUS TOPICS IN UNITED STATES HISTORY

Dickinson's American Historical Fiction. Metuchen, N.J.: Scarecrow Press, 1986. Virginia B. Gerhardstein.

How to Find Your Family Roots: The Comprehensive Guide to Tracing Your Ancestors Throughout the World. New York: McGraw-Hill, 1977.

American Family History: A Historical Bibliography. Santa Barbara, Cal.: ABC-Clio, 1984.

Biographical Dictionary of American Sports. Westport, Conn.: Greenwood Press, 1987–1989. David L. Porter, ed.

The History of American Education. Northbrook, Ill.: AHM Publishing, 1976. Jurgen Herbst, comp.

Bibliography of North American Folklore and Folksong. New York: Dover Publications, 1961. Charles Haywood, ed.

Encyclopedia of American Agricultural History. Westport, Conn.: Greenwood Press, 1975. Edwin I. Schapsmeier and Frederick H. Schapsmeier.

A Subject Bibliography of the History of American Higher Education. Westport, Conn.: Greenwood Press, 1984. Mark Beach, comp.

Nuclear America: A Historical Bibliography. Santa Barbara, Cal.: ABC-Clio, 1984.

The History of Science and Technology in the United States: A Critical and Selective Bibliography. New York: Garland, 1982. Marc Rothenberg, ed.

The Craft of Public History: An Annotated Select Bibliography. Westport, Conn.: Greenwood Press, 1983. David F. Trask and Robert W. Pomeroy III.

VIII. Sources for Historical Statistics

A. World Statistical Data

Historical Tables, 58 B.C.–A.D. 1978. New York: St. Martin's Press, 1979. Sigfrid H. Steinberg.

Statistics Sources. Detroit: Gale, 1982. Paul Wasserman and Jacqueline Bernero.

The International Almanac of Electoral History. Washington, D.C.: Congressional Quarterly, 1991. Thomas Mackie and Richard Rose.

Statistical Yearbooks: An Annotated Bibliography of the General Statistical Yearbooks of Major Political Subdivisions of the World. Washington, D.C.: Library of Congress, 1953.

Demographic Yearbook. New York: United Nations Statistical Office, 1949–present. Annual.

Population Index. Princeton, N.J.: Office of Population Research, 1935–present.

Statistical Yearbook. New York: United Nations Statistical Office, 1949–present.

B. European Statistical Data

European Historical Statistics, 1750–1975. New York: Facts on File, 1980. B. R. Mitchell.

European Political Facts, 1918–1973. New York: St. Martin's Press, 1978. Christopher Cook and John Paxton.

The Gallup International Public Opinion Polls. [France: 1939, 1944–1975] New York: Random House, 1976. George H. Gallup.

C. African, Asian, Latin American, and Middle Eastern Statistical Data

International Historical Statistics: Africa and Asia. New York: New York University Press, 1982. Brian R. Mitchell.

Statistical Abstract of Latin America. Los Angeles: U.C.L.A. Center of Latin American Studies, 1973–present. James W. Wilkie, ed.

International Historical Statistics: The Americas and Australasia. Detroit, Mich.: Gale, 1983. B.R. Mitchell, ed.

The Arab World, Turkey and the Balkans, 1878–1914: A Handbook of Historical Statistics. Boston, Mass.: G. K. Hall, 1982. Justin McCarthy, ed.

D. British Statistical Data

National Income, Expenditures and Output of the United Kingdom, 1855–1965. Cambridge: Cambridge University Press, 1972. C. H. Feinstein.

Annual Abstract of Statistics. London: Central Statistical Office of Great Britain, 1915/1928–present.

British Labour Statistics: Historical Abstract, 1886–1968. London: Great Britain Department of Employment and Productivity, 1971.

Abstract of British Historical Statistics. Cambridge: Cambridge University Press, 1976. B. R. Mitchell.

The British Voter: An Atlas and Survey Since 1885. London: Batsford, 1981. M. Kinnear.

British Political Facts, 1900–1979. New York: St. Martin's Press, 1980. David Butler and Ann Sloman.

The Gallup International Public Opinion Polls. [Britain, 1937–1975] New York: Random House, 1976. George H. Gallup.

British Historical Statistics. Cambridge: Cambridge University Press, 1988. B. R. Mitchell, ed.

E. United States and Canadian Statistical Data

Historical Statistics of the United States, Colonial Times to 1970. Washington, D.C.: Bureau of the Census, 1976.

Statistical Abstract of the United States. Washington, D.C.: Government Printing Office, 1878–present. Annual.

Bureau of the Census Catalog of Publications, 1790–1972. Washington, D.C.: Bureau of the Census, 1974.

American Statistics Index . . . : A Complete Guide and Index to the Statistical Publications of the United States Government. Washington, D.C.: Congressional Information Service, 1973–present.

Federal Population Censuses 1790–1890: A Catalogue of Microfilm Copies of the Schedules. Washington, D.C.: National Archives Trust Fund Board, 1979. Catalogs of the 1900 and 1910 censuses were published in 1978 and 1982.

The Gallup Poll. New York: Random House and Scholarly Resources, 1935–present. George H. Gallup.

Historical Statistics of Canada. Ottawa: Statistics Canada, 1983. M. C. Urquhart.

IX. Guides to Photographs, Microfilms, Microforms, Movies, Recordings, and Oral History

Guide to Microforms in Print: Author, Title. Westport, Conn.: Meckler, 1985. Annual since 1961. Also see:

Guide to Microforms in Print: Subject. Westport, Conn.: Meckler, 1985. Annual since 1961. Now published by K.G. Saur Verlag, Munich.

Catalogue of National Archives Microfilm Publications. Washington, D.C.: N.A.R.S., 1974–present.

List of National Archives Microfilm Publications, 1947–1974. Washington, D.C.: National Archives and Records Service, 1974. Supplemented by:

Supplementary List of National Archives Publications, 1974–1982. Washington, D.C.: N.A.R.S., 1982.

Subject Guide to Microforms in Print. Washington, D.C.: Microcard Editions, 1962–present. Albert J. Diaz, ed.

Library of Congress Catalogue: Motion Pictures and Filmstrips. Washington, D.C.: Library of Congress, 1953–1972.

Library of Congress Catalogue: Music and Phonorecords. Washington, D.C.: Library of Congress, 1953–present. Annual.

The Oral History Collection of Columbia University. New York: Colum-

bia University Oral History Research Office, 1979. Elizabeth Mason
and Louis M. Starr.

Oral History in the United States: A Directory. New York: Oral History
Association, 1971. Gary L. Shumway, comp. Locates and describes
oral history collections.

*Oral History Index: An International Directory of Oral History Inter-
views.* London: Meckler, 1990.

Picture Sources. New York: Special Libraries Association, 1983. Ernest
H. Robl, ed.

Microform Research Collections. Meckler, 1984, 2nd ed. Suzanne Cates
Dodson, ed.

*Pamphlets in American History: A Bibliographical Guide to the Micro-
film Collections.* Sanford, N.C.: Microfilming Corp. of America,
1979–1983. 4v.

Newspapers on Microfilm: United States, 1948–1983. Washington,
D.C.: Library of Congress, 1984.

X. Guides to Dissertations, Archives, and Manuscripts

Dissertation Abstracts International. Ann Arbor, Mich.: University Microfilms, 1938–present. Annual.

A Guide to Archives and Manuscripts in the United States. New Haven,
Conn.: Yale University Press, 1965. Philip C. Hamer, ed.

The National Union Catalog of Manuscript Collections. Washington,
D.C.: Library of Congress, 1962+.

XI. History Databases

The following indexes can be searched by computer. If any of them are
available in your library, ask for help in determining how they may be of
use to you in your research. Note that most databases do not include
material published before the 1970s. Be sure to note the time period of
the database.

Historical Abstracts. Lists and describes *articles* on all but United
States and Canadian history. Coverage: 1973 or later. Corresponds to the
printed source of the same name listed in section VII, C. of this appendix.

America: History and Life. Lists and describes *articles* on United States
and Canadian history. Coverage: 1964 or later. Corresponds to the printed
source of the same name listed in section VII, O. of this appendix.

Biography and Genealogy Master Index. An index to over three million
biographies contained in biographical dictionaries. Most useful for infor-

mation on persons who are not described in the major biography collections. The printed version is listed in section II, A. of this appendix.
Histline. Lists sources on the history of medicine. Coverage: 1970+.
The Magazine Index. A microfilmed index covering articles in several hundred *popular* periodicals. Covers the last five years only. Similar to the printed source *Reader's Guide to Periodical Literature* listed in section IV, B. of this appendix.
National Newspaper Index. An index to newspaper articles in several of the major U.S. newspapers. Coverage: 1979+.

Other databases that may be of use in history research are:

> Infotrac
> Periodical Abstracts
> Index to United Nations Documents and Publications
> Legaltrac
> MLA International Bibliography Database
> Newsbank
> PAIS
> Sociofile
> Statistics Masterfile
> WorldCat

Be sure to ask the librarian how to use these databases and how they might help your research.

Useful Information
for the Historian

Historical Sources in Your Own Backyard

Some of the most rewarding kinds of historical research concerns people, events, and places that you can almost reach out and touch. The history of your family, of the town you grew up in, or of events that shaped your parents' lives can be uncovered not only in a library but in a nearby museum or in a local history archive filled with old photographs, land deeds, birth registers, and personal correspondence. Every state in the United States and every province in Canada has its own historical society with a library of books, photographs, and documents on the state's history. Every city and most towns, even small ones, have a historical society or a museum where they keep the documents and artifacts (for example, objects like a millstone or a carriage) that tell the story of the town's past.

Wherever your school is located, from downtown Manhattan to rural Nebraska, you are probably not more than a short drive from a local history archive. If your research concerns the town or area where your school is located, look up the address of the local historical society and visit it. One of the most enjoyable aspects of history research is to hold in your hand an actual document or artifact that makes the past come alive—a 150-year-old land deed, a photograph of the center of town in 1890, a record player from 1918, a letter from a mother to her daughter written in 1838.

If you live or go to school in a large city or if you want to research the history of a county or an area of a state, many records are available to you. Each state (each province in Canada) and each county within that state will have its own archive of historical materials. Each city will have at least one such archive. Cities and towns also have private historical societies. There are thousands of state, county, and local museums and archives. The best way to locate the major archives is to look them up in *Directory of Historical Organizations in the United States and Canada.* This work is published by the American Association for State and Local History, and the most recent volume is edited by Mary Bray Wheeler. This directory lists many hundreds of organizations. It has an index that arranges organizations alphabetically by the name of the place whose history they record. The archives are also listed alphabetically by subject if their collection of documents or artifacts is specialized in some way— say a town that was an important battlefield in the Civil War. The name, address, and telephone number of each organization is listed along with a brief description of the kind of materials it contains.

Research and Study Guides in History

If you wish to consult a history study guide written for more advanced students, here is a list of some publications.

Wood Gray, *Historian's Handbook: A Key to the Study and Writing of History.* Boston: Houghton Mifflin, 1964.
Norman Cantor and Richard Schneider, *How to Study History.* New York: T. Y. Crowell, 1967.
Roberts Daniels, *Studying History: How and Why.* Englewood Cliffs, N.J.: Prentice-Hall, 1972.
Robert Shafer, *A Guide to Historical Method.* Homewood, Ill.: Dorsey, 1980.

Grammar and Style Manuals

If you know that your background in grammar and composition is weak, or if you need more specific information concerning report writing, here are a few manuals that should help.

Sheridan Baker, *The Complete Stylist and Handbook*. New York: Harper & Row, 1984.
Jacques Barzun and Henry Graff, *The Modern Researcher*. New York: Harcourt Brace Jovanovich, 1985.
University of Chicago Press, *The Chicago Manual of Style*. Chicago: University of Chicago Press, 1982.
Kate L. Turabian, *Student's Guide for Writing College Papers*. Chicago: University of Chicago Press, 1977.

Call Numbers: The Library of Congress System
The identification system of the Library of Congress divides the major subject classifications by letter. The following are the Library of Congress subject categories and their respective letter designations.

A General works
B Philosophy, psychology, religion
C Auxiliary sciences of history
D General and Old World history
E American (Western Hemisphere) history
F American history (continued)
G Geography, anthropology, customs, sports
H Social sciences, economics, socialism
J Political science, international law
K Law
L Education
M Music
N Fine arts
P Language, literature
Q Science
R Medicine
S Agriculture
T Technology
U Military science
V Naval science
Z Bibliography, library science

Each letter group is broken down further by the addition of a second letter and then by numbers. Here are some of the breakdowns of the categories D, E, and F, which deal with history.

D   General history
DA   Great Britain
         20–690 England

700–745 Wales
750–890 Scotland
900–995 Ireland

DB   Austria-Hungary
DC   France
DD   Germany
DE   Classical antiquity
DF   Greece
DG   Italy
DH-DJ Netherlands
       DH   1–207 Belgium and Holland
       DH   401–811 Belgium
       DH   901–925 Luxemburg (grand duchy)
       DJ   Holland
DK   Russia
        1–272 Russia (general)
        401–441 Poland
        445–465 Finland
        750–891 Russia in Asia
DL   Scandinavia
        1–85 Scandinavia (general)
        101–291 Denmark
        301–398 Iceland
        401–596 Norway
        601–991 Sweden
DP   Spain and Portugal
        1–402 Spain
        501–900 Portugal
DQ   Switzerland
DR   Turkey and the Balkan States
DS   Asia
DT   Africa
DU   Australia and Oceania
DX   Gypsies

E   America (General) and United States (General)
      11–143 America (general)
      31–45 North America (general)
      51–99 Indians of North America
      101–135 Discovery of America
      151–810 United States

151–185 General history and description
185 Afro-Americans in the United States
186–199 Colonial period
201–298 Revolution
351–364 War of 1812
401–415 War with Mexico
441–453 Slavery
458–655 Civil War
482–489 Confederate States
714–735 War with Spain

F   United States (local) and America except the United States
1–970 United States (local)
1001–1140 British North America, Canada,
    Newfoundland
1201–1392 Mexico
1401–1419 Latin America (general)
1421–1577 Central America
1601–2151 West Indies
2201–2239 South America (general)
2251–2299 Colombia
2301–2349 Venezuela
2351–2471 Guiana: British, Dutch, French
2501–2659 Brazil
2661–2699 Paraguay
2701–2799 Uruguay
2801–3021 Argentine Republic
3051–3285 Chile
3301–3359 Bolivia
3401–3619 Peru
3701–3799 Ecuador

Thus a volume whose call number begins DK 408 deals with Polish history, and one which begins E 451 is about the history of slavery in the United States.

Call Numbers: The Dewey Decimal System
The Dewey system is a decimal system. There are ten main subject headings, each containing 100 different numbers:

000–099 General works
100–199 Philosophy
200–299 Religion

300–399 Social sciences
400–499 Language
500–599 Pure science
600–699 Technology
700–799 The arts
800–899 Literature
900–999 History

Each of the main subject divisions is itself divided into ten sections of ten units each. The divisions of history are:

900–909 General history
910–919 Geography, travel, description
920–929 Biography
930–939 Ancient history
940–949 European history
950–959 Asian history
960–969 African history
970–979 North American history
980–989 South American history
990–999 Other regions of the world

Each of these divisions is further divided into ten parts. The divisions of 970 to 979 (North American history), for example, are as follows:

970 General North American history
971 Canadian history
972 Mexican and Caribbean history
973 General United States history
974 Northeastern states, U.S.
975 Southeastern states, U.S.
976 South-central states, U.S.
977 North-central states, U.S.
978 Western states, U.S.
979 Far-western states, U.S. and Alaska

Thus a volume whose call number begins with 934 deals with ancient history, and one that begins with 978 is concerned with the history of one or more of the western states of the United States.

Common Abbreviations Used in Footnotes, Bibliographies, Catalogs, and Reference Books

anon.   anonymous
app.   appendix

art.	article (plural, arts.)
b.	born
bk.	book (plural, bks.)
bull.	bulletin
c.	copyright
ca.	*circa*, about, approximately. Used with approximate dates, e.g., "ca. 1804."
cf.	*confer*, compare. Used only when the writer wishes the reader to compare two or more works.
ch. or chap.	chapter (plural, chaps.)
col.	column (plural, cols.)
comp.	compiler (plural, comps.)
d.	died
diss.	dissertation
ed.	edition, editor (plural eds.)
e.g.	*exempli gratia*, for example
enl.	enlarged
et al.	*et alia*, and others
et seq.	*et sequens*, and the following
fac.	facsimile
fig.	figure (plural, figs.)
ibid.	*ibidem*, in the same place
id.	*idem*, the same (person)
i.e.	*id est*, that is
ill.	illustrated, illustration
infra	below (referring to a later point in the work)
l. or ll.	line(s)
loc. cit.	*loco citato*, in the place cited (referring to the same passage cited in an immediately previous footnote)
MS	manuscript (plural, MSS)
n.	note, footnote (plural, nn.)
n.d.	no date (of publication is given)
no.	number (plural, nos.)
n.p.	no place (of publication) or no publisher (is given)
n.s.	new series
o.p.	out of print
op. cit.	*opere citato*, in the work cited
o.s.	old series
p.	page (plural, pp.)
par.	paragraph (plural, pars.)
passim	here and there (throughout the work cited)

pseud.	pseudonym
pt.	part (plural, pts.)
q.v.	*quod vide*, which see
rev.	revised
sc.	scene
sic	so, thus (Enclosed in brackets to indicate an error or unusual statement in a quotation.)
supp.	supplement (plural, supps.)
supra	above (referring to an earlier point in the work)
trans.	translator
viz.	*videlicet,* namely
v. or vol.	volume (plural, vols.)
vs.	*versus,* against